GOOD MEN

GOOD MEN

The Lives and Philanthropy of
Irwin A. and Robert D. Goodman

DOUG MOE

Parallel Press / University of Wisconsin–Madison Libraries

Parallel Press
University of Wisconsin–Madison Libraries
728 State Street
Madison, Wisconsin 53706
parallelpress.library.wisc.edu

ISBN 978-1-934795-63-7

Design and production, University Marketing and Communications,
University of Wisconsin–Madison

Photos are from the personal collection of
Irwin A. and Robert D. Goodman, unless otherwise noted.
Cover photo by Andy Manis.

FOREWORD

Irwin and Bob Goodman were among the first people whose names I heard when Kelly and I came to Madison in 1976.

It seemed everyone knew the Goodmans, respected them as State Street businessmen, and appreciated their philanthropy across the city.

That was certainly true inside the University of Wisconsin athletic department. I was an assistant to Bill Cofield at the time, and on the road so much recruiting that I even missed the basketball banquet at the end of the first season, in spring 1977. There was no down time in recruiting then. Now we have periods when you can't go on the road. Not then. If you weren't out recruiting, you could be sure Indiana and Michigan were. I was gone a lot.

Kelly went to that first banquet by herself. It was at the Memorial Union. She told me later that when the banquet was over, a man approached her with a friendly smile and immediately started apologizing for having stared at her during dinner. He couldn't help it, he said, she was that beautiful.

Of course, that was Bob Goodman. Kelly hadn't noticed the staring, and she smiled and introduced herself. Bob recognized pretty quickly that she wasn't wearing a diamond ring. We hadn't been able to afford a diamond when we got engaged a few years earlier. Then, when we came to Madison, a house was more important. We bought a house on the G.I. Bill at the corner of Tokay Boulevard and Segoe Road.

Bob told Kelly that we should come into the store, and he'd set us up with a diamond. That's what happened. He gave us a good deal, and subsequently, all our jewelry purchases were with the Goodmans.

Going to Goodman's was an easy decision, and not only because we liked Irwin and Bob. It seemed like every time we turned around, we'd hear they were sponsoring a civic event, or donating to a worthy cause. They didn't do it for personal recognition. They did it because it was the right thing to do. As you will learn in this book, their mother taught them about giving back to the community. They took it to heart. Elsewhere in the book, former mayor Dave Cieslewicz says Irwin and Bob set the gold standard for philanthropy in Madison. Who would argue?

I always appreciated that while Bob and Irwin were generous contributors to UW athletics, they didn't try to tell us our business. Sometimes people will ask a thousand questions about recruiting, or why is this guy playing, and that guy not playing? It's something coaches understand. The Goodmans—who were certainly in a position to ask any questions they cared to—kept it cheerful and light. They might ask just generally how the team was going to do. In those early days, when we weren't really setting the world on fire, they'd find something good we were doing and focus on that.

When I was named head coach of the Badgers in 2001, the Goodmans called us in Milwaukee with congratulations. Kelly spoke with them. They were happy for us, and wanted to let us know.

It was a kind gesture, and typical of them. At some point after Irwin and Bob died—within nine months of each other, in 2009 and 2010—we heard from John Hayes, who bought the jewelry store from Bob and Irwin, and operates it very much in their spirit.

John and his wife, Cathy, had an antique ring that had come from Bob's desk, and had been a favorite of his. They thought Bob and Irwin would want Kelly to have it. We were touched.

Just how many people were touched by the Goodmans' good will and philanthropy can be found in the pages that follow.

Bo Ryan
Head men's basketball coach
University of Wisconsin–Madison

ILLUSTRATION BY EARL J. MADDEN

GOOD MEN
The Lives and Philanthropy of Irwin A. and Robert D. Goodman

CHAPTER 1
A Community Pool, and So Much More

The first day of September was one of the last hot days of what had been a hot summer 2011 in Madison, Wisconsin.

School was still a few days off, and that afternoon, a great many kids and a number of their parents were splashing in a large swimming pool on the city's south side. Those not swimming were standing in line for one of the two water slides or lounging in chairs and enjoying the sun. It was a happy scene.

Two boys, 12-year-old classmates at Wright School in Madison, one black, one white, one with goggles and one without, hauled themselves from the pool, grinning and a little out of breath.

"How many times have you been here this summer?" they were asked.

A journalist had approached.

"At least twenty," one said. He pointed at his friend.

"He's been more."

"Do you know who Bob and Irwin Goodman were?"

The boy with the goggles had pushed them to the top of his head.

"We know they built the pool," he said.

"Know anything else about them?"

The boys looked at each other and shrugged.

It is likely few of the several hundred people enjoying the Goodman Pool on Madison's south side that day knew much more than the young Wright students about the brothers who gave the pool, and so much else, to the city they adopted as their own shortly after relocating from their native Minnesota in the 1930s.

Certainly, in one sense, nearly everyone in Madison knew the Goodmans. Long before their philanthropy made headlines, Bob and Irwin were recognized as successful State Street jewelers, and Bob was a decorated local athlete. Both men were naturally friendly—Bob, especially, was gregarious, always smiling, with an encyclopedic memory for names—and the brothers often got out and about to Rotary meetings and University of Wisconsin sports events. They enjoyed local restaurants and walking on Madison's beautiful isthmus.

But on a deeper level, Bob and Irwin Goodman were hard to know. They lived together in a modest apartment in downtown Madison and were as devoted to one another as they had once been to the mother who had a tremendous influence on their lives. In some ways they exemplified a generation that honored achievement but did not boast, that worked hard and didn't complain. Irwin wouldn't complain when people called him "Irv," a nickname he never really liked. It was a generation, too, that believed in giving back to the communities in which one lived, while allowing private lives, one's own and others, to remain private.

Bob and Irwin were private people, but in 1993, when their generosity as philanthropists was really beginning to be appreciated in Madison—many of the Goodmans' early charitable gifts were given anonymously—*Capital Times* feature writer Rob Zaleski managed to secure one of the only press interviews the brothers ever granted.

Zaleski began his piece by saying how difficult it had been to get the Goodmans to agree to be featured in the newspaper.

"Irv Goodman," Zaleski wrote, "one of the most gentle, laid-back, unflappable guys in the history of the planet, has not had a decent night's sleep all week."

Why was Irwin having trouble sleeping? Zaleski ex-

plained: "Truth is, Irv is worried about this story."

In the end, Zaleski's piece painted a delightful picture of Bob and Irwin Goodman: loving brothers who never married, who enjoyed a joke (especially Bob), devout vegetarians (especially Irwin), rabid sports fans, successful businessmen and philanthropists. Zaleski made note of "the $100,000 they recently gave to the United Way for a special fund to help the most desperate in the community."

But Zaleski was right to begin his profile with his subjects' reticence. It was never about personal publicity for the Goodmans, even if that publicity was unavoidable as their donations to the city they loved almost like it was family became ever more generous. The Goodmans were smart and savvy enough to know public philanthropy brings complications beyond publicity.

Giving on a large scale is never as easy as it might seem, and certainly that was true of the swimming pool that may stand as the Goodmans' most significant gift to Madison. The brothers thought so. Others might point to the Goodman Community Center on the city's east side, but then why argue over which of two shining jewels is brightest? The point is Bob and Irwin loved the pool, loved that they had been able to help, in a large way, to make it happen.

Maybe that had something to do with the fact that Madison had been trying, in fits and starts, to build a community swimming pool for more than 50 years when the Goodmans first became seriously involved in the spring of 2003.

More than half a century earlier, in the 1940s, the idea of a public pool in Madison had been floated, but the idea was rejected in large part because the city had numerous public beaches, and the lakes, at that time, were reasonably clean. As the decades rolled on, swimming in the lakes became far less desirable.

Smaller cities surrounding Madison realized that the polluted lakes were no longer a good swimming option. Sun Prairie, Middleton and Monona built community pools. Madison did not.

One early effort, in 1974, came and went quickly. A Madison alder, Michael Ley, introduced a resolution that requested $7,000 for a study of the costs and benefits of

The city of Madison had been trying to build a community pool for more than half a century, without success, when Irwin and Bob Goodman made the lead gift that led to the Goodman Pool, which opened in 2006.

CAPITAL NEWSPAPERS ARCHIVE

a public pool. He got nowhere, and said, "The one thing I've learned in public life is everyone wants services but no one wants to pay for them."

Of course, some were quick to say there were plenty of pools, which was true, but they were private. In the early '90s, when the idea of a community pool was first seriously discussed in Madison, a family membership at Ridgewood Pool, a typical private pool in the Orchard Ridge neighborhood on the west side, required a $600 stock purchase and a $600 annual membership fee. What it meant was that Madison had public pools only for people of means.

It seemed a shame for that to be the case in progressive Madison, and by 1990, a serious fund-raising effort for a public pool had begun. Local businessman Bill Graham was on point, and Paul Soglin, beginning a second extended stint as mayor, said city funds could be utilized as well. A study recommended Olin-Turville Park, across from the Dane County Coliseum and not far from Lake Monona, as the pool site.

Despite raising nearly $900,000 in private donations by February 1992, and with a who's who of Madison movers and shakers behind it, the Olin-Turville pool never happened. An organized opposition, charging that the public had not had sufficient input in the process, succeeded in getting a referendum on the April 1992 ballot that not only scuttled the Olin-Park pool but put in place an ordinance requiring public approval of all projects costing more than $500,000 in parks next to navigable waters.

It was a bitter defeat for pool enthusiasts, and as the 1990s progressed, many of the pool's biggest supporters gave up hope. Rob Zaleski, the *Capital Times* writer who had profiled the Goodmans in 1993, and who authored more than a dozen columns in support of a community pool, wrote the following in 2001: "It has finally dawned on me—understand, as a rule journalists are rather slow—that a public swimming pool ain't gonna happen here. Not tomorrow, not 10 years from tomorrow."

Less than two years later, in 2003, Bob and Irwin Goodman would read another newspaper article, an interview with a new Madison mayor, Dave Cieslewicz, in which he listed a public pool among his priorities. Their

Irwin (left) and Bob Goodman in front of the their jewelry store on State Street. They owned the store for more than 60 years, and loved walking on State Street and all of Madison's beautiful isthmus.

reading of that story would begin a process—a difficult, complex process—that would lead to Madison finally getting its first public pool.

Anyone who knew the Goodmans couldn't have been surprised when the first public word came of their interest in helping to build a swimming pool. Athletics of all kinds had always been a big part of Bob's and Irwin's lives. As young men, they were both excellent athletes. Later in life, their love of sports would be reflected in generous gifts to the University of Wisconsin athletic department, most notably donating $500,000 to help build a park for women's softball. The program was instituted at UW–Madison in 1994 and the Goodman Diamond, located near Lake Mendota behind the Nielsen Tennis

Bob Goodman makes the ceremonial first pitch at the opening of the Goodman Diamond in 1999. Bob and Irwin's gift made the UW women's softball complex possible.

Stadium, opened in March 1999. Athletic Director Pat Richter and Chancellor David Ward made remarks at the ribbon cutting preceding a game between Wisconsin and Loyola.

Bob Goodman threw out the ceremonial first pitch.

Richter—on crutches following hip surgery—laughed and said, "Bob was just beaming. I think he wanted to start playing again."

Bob said, "This is not for Irv and Bob Goodman. This is for the university and about the kids. That's what this is all about."

Irwin was not feeling well enough to attend, and no one who knew the brothers was surprised when Bob said he couldn't stay for the game—actually a doubleheader—because he had to get back home and look after Irwin.

Still, it was a magical day at the new diamond. The Badgers swept Loyola. Bob, before leaving, said, "It's a dream come true. I'm just so proud. Hopefully every day the team plays the sun will shine like it did today."

A week later, a letter arrived that the brothers would cherish for years to come. It was signed by each member of the UW women's softball team.

"Hopefully in the future," the young women wrote, "we can make a difference in someone else's life by simulating your kindness and generosity to others." They concluded, "The impact that you have had on our lives will never be forgotten."

The Goodmans were regulars as spectators at UW sporting events throughout their lives, but not everyone knew that they were also fine athletes themselves—Bob in particular. They had fallen hard for sports as kids growing up in St. Paul, and not even their parents' lack of enthusiasm for their participation could dissuade them.

"They were always real good athletes," recalled their childhood friend Jack Stevenson. Irwin was accomplished in track and field, while Bob played football, baseball and hockey. Sports were central to their lives.

That was true long after they were no longer participating themselves. Bob and Irwin lived in a modest downtown apartment and would travel across town to find a bargain when shopping. One of the very few luxuries they allowed themselves was a high-tech television on which to watch sporting events.

"They had a flat screen TV about half the size of a living room wall," their friend Bob Pricer said.

Pricer, a UW School of Business professor, helped Bob and Irwin with some business dealings, becoming in the process a trusted friend. He continued, "They didn't buy material things. But sports were a huge part of their lives until the end. They followed all sports. One of their disappointments with me was that I couldn't sit down and talk Brewers' batting averages with them. They would talk about batting averages and the changes in the pitching rotation."

Pricer first met Bob and Irwin in the 1990s, when they sought his help in selling their State Street jewelry store. The sale, to longtime employee John Hayes, happened in 1998, a few years before the pool project heated up. The sale of the store (after six decades) was significant, a defining moment that might naturally have led the Goodmans to consider their legacy.

Part of the legacy, of course, was the store itself, and the Goodmans were confident it was in good hands with Hayes

The State Street jewelry store had been in the Goodman family since 1933. The family owned a chain of jewelry stores around the Midwest and one of them was on State Street in Madison. Irwin actually had a significant role in the family acquiring the store. He'd come to Madison as a track athlete at the University of Minnesota, fallen in love with Madison, and convinced his father and uncles to purchase the store at 220 State Street.

"It was a failing jewelry store," said John Hayes, who learned the history from Bob and Irwin.

After graduating in 1937 with a business administration degree, Irwin went to work at the store.

"The manager, whom I don't believe was a family relation, didn't really manage the store," Hayes said. "He was off playing golf. So Irwin took over the store."

A year later, Irwin convinced his younger brother Bob—who had started at Minnesota but then transferred to UW–Madison—to join him in the business. For the next 60 years, they would make a formidable team.

Irwin worked largely in the office, doing the books, the inventory and the buying. Bob was out front, cultivating relationships.

John Hayes said, "Irwin was the books and management and business side of it. Bob was the front man and the salesman. He was charismatic. He would meet somebody and then not see them for five years and still know their name."

Hayes continued, "Their roles at the store fit their personalities perfectly. Bob could talk to anybody and was comfortable with everyone who came in the store."

Hayes found their business philosophy to be both simple and profound.

"Irwin always told me there's three ways to make money in business," Hayes said. "You buy right: get the right inventory and the right product mix at the right prices. You sell right: sell the product at a fair price with a good margin. You pay your bills right: any time you can take advantage of an early payment discount, you do so. You set up relationships with vendors so that when you need something they're there to back you up. You weave those things together to create a good business model."

At the core of the business was an inherent decency that guided them in everything they did. "Their mantra," Hayes said, "was to treat people as you would like to be treated. Be honest and fair to people."

Bob and Irwin found a kindred soul in Hayes, who six months after being hired in 1983 was promoted to sales manager. It was the brothers' good feeling toward Hayes that finally allowed them, a dozen years later, to begin thinking seriously about selling the store. The sale was finalized in 1998.

At the core of the business was an inherent decency that guided them in everything they did. "Their mantra," Hayes said, "was to treat people as you would like to be treated. Be honest and fair with people."

With the store in good hands, the other, and perhaps greater, piece of the Goodmans' legacy came to the fore. Their philanthropic instincts, never far from the surface, began to take on a greater urgency. Irwin, who of the two brothers was the planner, began to realize it was possible for them to make significantly large gifts, and that those gifts would in turn establish a legacy. It was important to Irwin for the Goodman name to live on.

In November 1998, Bob and Irwin agreed to another rare newspaper interview, this one with Scott Milfred of the *Wisconsin State Journal*. They liked Milfred, who lived near them downtown. The story ran on page one on a Sunday, by far the paper's biggest circulation day.

"The Goodmans still keep a rigorous schedule," Milfred wrote, despite the fact that Irwin was then 83, and Bob 79. "They rise at 5 a.m. every day in their third floor,

John Hayes (left), purchased the jewelry store from Bob and Irwin after working for them for many years, and gaining their trust.

group founded in 1948 that published a bi-monthly magazine called *Health Science*.

In the front of the magazine was a description of Natural Hygiene: "A philosophy and set of principles and practices based on science that lead to an extraordinary level of personal health and happiness." The recommended diet: "A whole-food, plant-based diet of fresh un-cooked fruits and vegetables; steamed vegetables; baked potatoes; squashes; raw, unsalted nuts; and whole grains, designed to meet individual needs."

Susan Hill of Madison was a cousin of the Goodmans and saw them with some frequency. "When we had them over to our house," Hill recalled, "Irwin would say, 'Now, what are you going to prepare?'"

Irwin wasn't trying to be difficult, but he would make it clear that the brothers' diet did not include salt or pepper or seasoning of any kind. Friends and restaurants were generally happy to accommodate them.

The Memorial Union on the UW–Madison campus, where the Goodmans regularly attended a variety of functions, prepared special dishes for the Goodmans and even named one in their honor. There was a plaque with Bob's and Irwin's names at the Ponderosa restaurant on the west side—the brothers loved the restaurant's salad bar—and they also frequented the restaurant Himal Chuli on State Street, which featured many vegetarian meals.

It was Irwin, considering longevity, who insisted on the diet. Their mother had died at 66, their father at 70. Irwin thought Natural Hygiene was the key to a long life. Bob was less enthusiastic, but expressed his feelings with characteristic good humor. "We may not live forever," he'd say, "but it will feel like it."

The majority of Scott Milfred's 1998 *Wisconsin State Journal* article was devoted to the Goodmans' philanthropy. Leslie Ann Howard, president of the United Way of Dane County, was quoted: "They've adopted the community as their ward. They really feel a responsibility. Much as a person would take care of a child, they're taking care of Madison."

A sidebar to the page one story was headlined: "The Goodmans' Gifts Are All Over Madison." The sidebar noted more than a dozen separate gifts, many of them provided

Wilson Street apartment overlooking Lake Monona."

The brothers loved the location and had been there nearly three decades. When they moved in, in 1970, the colorful *Wisconsin State Journal* sports columnist Joseph "Roundy" Coughlin mentioned their new home in a particularly vivid item: "Bob and Irwin Goodman have moved into the Town House on West Wilson Street. The jewelry daily double said it is the most beautiful sight you can find looking out onto Lake Monona and the surrounding views. They said when the moon shines on the lake it looks like a million diamonds are shining on the water."

Always up early, as Milfred noted in 1998, the brothers typically began their day with exercise.

"Their routine starts with weightlifting," Milfred wrote, "pushups and frequent walks around the nearby Monona Terrace Convention Center. Three times a week they catch a ride to a fitness center. Bob walks on treadmill and rides an exercise bike. Irwin walks laps around the pool."

By 1998, a keen concern about their health had been an integral part of the brothers' lives for three decades.

Beginning in 1967, the brothers were members of the American Natural Hygiene Society, a Tampa-based

Having lived in Madison since the 1930s, Irwin (left) and Bob regarded the city as family.

on an ongoing annual basis. It mentioned the UW–Madison women's softball diamond; $250,000 to start the Goodman Rotary Senior Fitness Fund; hundreds of thousands of dollars to the United Way of Dane County; and more.

The scope of their giving was already remarkable, but the decade following that article's publication would bring even more generous gifts, the most significant of the Goodmans' lives. Jewish causes were important to Bob and Irwin, and the brothers would donate $1.5 million to the Madison Jewish Community Council to buy 155 acres of land near Verona for a Jewish community campus. The Goodmans would also contribute $2 million toward a new home for an east side community center that, when completed, would become known as the Goodman Community Center.

And, at long last, they tackled the idea of a Madison community pool.

The election of the young, energetic Dave Cieslewicz as Madison mayor in 2003 was something Bob and Irwin had been following. They read both Madison daily papers. "Front to back," a friend recalled.

"They had followed Dave and liked what he had to

say about the city," Pricer said. "One day Irwin said to me, 'We like this new mayor. We like his vision, and we'd like to help him. He wants to build a pool, and we'd like to see if we can help get that done.'"

Pricer enlisted some help—notably Nino Amato, a longtime Madisonian and one time mayoral candidate who knew his way around Madison's nuanced politics—and discussions began to ensure that if and when the Goodmans made a significant gift for a pool, it would go as smoothly as possible. It may be hard to imagine a financial gift in the millions being welcomed with anything but open arms, but it can happen.

Irwin, meanwhile, big-hearted but savvy, too, had his own ideas about how the pool gift could best be made. He originally did not want their gift to be the "lead" gift, because he had learned it often meant they would be contacted again later for yet another large donation. In the end, when it became clear there would be no public pool without a lead gift from the Goodmans, Irwin agreed, while continuing to insist there be major involvement from others in the community.

Early on in the process, Irwin also set a condition—

brilliant, in hindsight—that pool construction needed to start within one year of the announcement of their gift.

"The Goodmans knew their community," Dave Cieslewicz said. "They saw what had happened when we tried to put the pool at Olin-Turville."

When discussions began again in 2003, it was clear to all that the right site for a public pool was critical to the project's success. Mayor Cieslewicz appointed an Ad Hoc Swimming Pool Committee which was tasked with choosing a site.

The site committee was announced the same day—June 24, 2004—Cieslewicz held a news conference to announce the Goodmans' $2 million lead gift for the swimming pool. Bob and Irwin did not attend, but the mayor made sure they received their due.

"They are making a bricks and mortar reality out of something that has been a community dream for decades," Cieslewicz said. "With their generous gift of $2 million, it is no longer a question of if we will build a pool. The questions now are when, where, and what will it look like."

Where to locate Madison's first public pool was never going to be an easy decision. The committee held regular meetings and received intense community input. Just about every neighborhood association in the city found reasons why their neighborhood would provide the best fit. Bob and Irwin were hopeful that one of the contenders, Franklin Field on the city's south side, would be chosen. They liked the area's economic and ethnic diversity and thought locating the pool there would be good for the city. Yet the brothers did not lobby publicly for that site. They were smart enough to realize such an effort by the lead donors might backfire. In the end, after many meetings and discussions, and after considering purchasing one of the existing pools in the city, the pool committee settled on the Franklin Field site as best for Madison's first community swimming pool.

There would be more hurdles to overcome—another referendum, and then the Goodmans would be asked, just as they had feared, to come up with significant additional funds—but in June, 2006, the Goodman Pool opened to great acclaim in the Franklin Field area that by

then had been renamed Goodman Park.

"During all this," Cieslewicz said of the brothers, "they were just the sweetest guys. They would call me occasionally—sometimes it wasn't even about the pool. They may have picked up the paper and realized I was having a tough time. And they would just call me up and give me a little pep talk. It was usually Bob, sometimes Irv. They'd say, 'We know you're busy, but we just wanted to call and say we think you're doing a good job.'"

Cieslewicz paused, recalling those conversations. "I would put down the phone with tears in my eyes."

Bob and Irwin had gotten a tour of the pool facility a day or two before the grand opening—Irwin was in a wheelchair by then—but on opening day they stayed home. Irwin wasn't up to it, and besides, being in that grand opening spotlight had never been their style.

"I think they set a gold standard for philanthropy in this community," Cieslewicz said. "They did it just right. They were incredibly generous but they were also smart businessmen. They didn't just give their money away willy-nilly. They did their research. They understood what they were giving money to and they set standards for accomplishment. There are different ways to do philanthropy. The Goodmans hit the sweet spot."

Once the pool was operating, the brothers would be driven by once or twice a month. It's easy to see the pool from Olin Avenue, and Bob's and Irwin's eyes would light up at all the happy splashing and commotion inside. The kids and their parents reflected—and continue to reflect—Madison's increasing racial diversity. The Goodmans had hoped it would be a pool for everyone, and so it is.

It should be noted that early on, during that first summer, organizers had been troubled by a lack of the diversity everyone hoped the Franklin Field site would provide. The answer was that many minority kids did not know how to swim. The Goodmans came forward with a $50,000 annual donation for swimming lessons, diversity flourished, and before too long the Goodman Pool had a team entered in the All-City Swim Meet.

It was yet another demonstration of what more than one person would say of Bob and Irwin over the years: Madison was their family.

CHAPTER 2

From Gutmann to Goodman; from Minnesota to Madison

They had real family, of course, and until their father traveled to the United States on an ocean liner, the name wasn't Goodman. It was Gutmann.

Imre Gutmann was the name that the man who came to be known as Harry Julius Goodman listed—or had listed for him by an employee of the shipping line—when he boarded the Augusta Victoria in Hamburg, Germany, on June 7, 1899. The first name on the ship's log is hard to read: it appears to be Imre.

His destination was New York City, and, eventually, St. Paul, Minnesota, where an older brother had been living since 1893. The brother's name was Albert Goodman. Harry—his name was likely Americanized as soon as he got to St. Paul—was 20 years old when he stepped aboard the ship in Hamburg in 1899. On boarding he was asked to declare how much money he had in his possession. The answer, recorded in the ship's log: $12.

On a later passport application, Harry would state that he was born in Russia, on March 11, 1879. He wrote the town name as Valdislawovo, which appears to be a derivation of Vladislavovas, in an area of Eastern Europe which over the years would find itself part of Poland and Lithuania as well as Russia. Wars and skirmishes and the passage of time meant shifting boundaries. The town's name changed, too: it would be called Neustadt-Schirwindt (when German) and then Kudirkos Naumiestis (when Lithuanian), the latter after a Lithuanian patriot, Vincas Kudirka, who lived there from 1895 to 1899. Whatever the name, it was never very big. The town's population in 2010—when it was part of Lithuania—was 1,911.

On various official documents over the years, Harry would list his home country as Germany, Poland, Russia or Lithuania, possibly reflecting the country that ruled the area at the given time he was filling out a document.

What's more certain is that when Albert Goodman, in 1893, and six years later, his younger brother, Harry, decided to immigrate to the United States, they were part of a large exodus of Jews from Eastern Europe eventually destined to land in America.

One immigrant who was born in their hometown of Vladislavov, and who left for the United States the same year as Albert Goodman (1893), became a well-known journalist in America.

The Goodmans, from left: Irwin, Harry, Belle and Bob. Eventually their parents followed Irwin and Bob to Madison.

Herman Bernstein was born in Vladislavov in 1876. After arriving in the United States he worked as a correspondent for the *New York Times* and *New York Herald*, covering the Russian Revolution and the Paris Peace Conference and in 1921 publishing a book, *The History of a Lie*, about the forgery of the "The Protocols of the Elders of Zion."

Many of the Jews who left Eastern Europe and landed in New York continued on to the American Midwest. A book on St. Paul, Minnesota, titled *Celebrate St. Paul: 150 Years of History*, described the migration in the late 19th century.

"As wages and living conditions in northern European countries improved," the book noted, "immigration from these places to the United States slackened. Simultaneously, conditions in eastern and southern Europe grew worse, which motivated more and more people to leave this area and seek a better life in America."

The book continued: "In St. Paul, the first significant indication of this change occurred on July 14, 1882, when 200 Jewish men, women and children, refugees from increased political and religious discrimination in Russia, arrived unannounced at the railroad depot." The book noted, "The Jews from Russia were among the first of many newcomers to St. Paul from eastern and southern Europe."

Albert Goodman—Bob's and Irwin's uncle—landed in St. Paul in 1893. Albert and Harry's parents, Isaac and Rivka Gutmann, never came to the United States, or at least they do not show up in any census. But it appears that members of Isaac and Rivka's family did, and may have been the first of Bob and Irwin's extended family to both live in the United States and work in the jewelry business.

Rivka's maiden name was Finkelstein, and the 1900 United States census shows Albert Goodman living in a home at 673 Cedar Avenue in St. Paul. The head of the household is identified on the census as Louis Finkelstein. He immigrated to the United States in 1870 and his occupation is listed as wholesale jeweler. It appears probable that Louis Finkelstein was Rivka's brother—and Albert's and Harry's uncle—and that Albert, listed as a "traveling agent," likely worked for him in the jewelry business.

The Finkelstein name is prominent in early St. Paul history. Moses Finkelstein—his relation if any to Louis is unclear—was named to the *Minnesota 150: People, Places and Other Things That Shaped Our State,* by the Minnesota Historical Society in 2007. Moses Finkelstein is identified as "a Lithuanian immigrant who arrived in St. Paul during the 1880s and quickly established himself as one of the city's most successful jewelers." Louis Finkelstein—who owned the home where Albert Goodman lived in 1900 and for whom Albert worked—was also a jeweler. Moses eventually went into the movie theater business and assembled one of the largest theater chains in the Midwest.

Although he came to the United States in 1899, stating he was coming to see his brother Albert in St. Paul, Harry Goodman—eventual father of Bob and Irwin—first shows up on the Minnesota census in 1905.

Much of what we know of him is gleaned from a document five years later, in a July 1910 application for a United States passport. Harry was then 31, and needed to return to Europe. "I am about to go abroad temporarily for the purpose of visiting my aged father who is sick in Germany," Harry wrote. "I intend to return to the United States within eight weeks."

It was on this passport application that Harry revealed his birth in Russia in March, 1879. He also noted that as of 1910, he was a resident of St. Paul, "where I follow the occupation of a jeweler."

He was living at 156 E. Seventh Street in St Paul, and described himself physically as follows: 5 feet, 5 inches tall, 180 pounds; sandy blond hair; gray eyes; prominent forehead; a nose and mouth he described as "regular," with a "square" chin.

Within four years of the trip to Germany to visit his ailing father, Harry, back in St. Paul, had met and married a St. Paul native. Her name was Belle Abrahamson.

Belle's father, Louis Abrahamson, was himself a native of Poland, born there in 1855. His 1939 news obituary in the St. Paul newspaper stated that Abrahamson came to the United States, and then to St. Paul, in 1878 when he was 23.

Although he came to the United States in 1899, stating he was coming to see his brother Albert in St. Paul, Harry Goodman – eventual father of Bob and Irwin – first shows up on the Minnesota census in 1905.

"Almost immediately upon coming to the city he went into the clothing business," the article stated, "opening a store on Kellogg Boulevard, which was then Third Street, near Market Street." The obituary stated that he remained in business in the same store until his retirement in 1932.

Abrahamson's religion seems to have been of great import to him. The article noted, "Throughout his residence in St. Paul he was interested in Jewish philanthropies and welfare organizations, and served as treasurer of several organizations which sent funds to Palestine or to European colleges for Jewish students.

"Among the St. Paul outstanding organizations to which he gave his services," the article continued, "are the Sons of Jacob synagogue at College and Wabash Streets,

Harry J. Goodman, immigrant from Eastern Europe, jeweler, and father of Irwin and Bob Goodman.

An exact wedding date for Harry J. Goodman and Belle Abrahamson is not known. Most likely it occurred between the fall of 1912, when Belle turned 18, and the summer of 1914.

Harry and Belle's first child, Irwin Arnold Goodman, was born July 1, 1915.

Nearly four years later, on June 28, 1919, a second son, Robert Dean Goodman, was born. The family of four showed up in the 1920 United States census. They were living at 681 Dayton Avenue in St. Paul. A few things stand out in the census. Harry now listed his native country as Germany and his native language as Hebrew. He also claimed to have become a naturalized United States citizen in 1905. That wasn't true, at least according to the passport application he filed in 1910. On that document, Harry stated that in 1909, he declared his "intention to become a citizen of the United States."

The census also reveals that Harry's younger brother, Theodore, was then living in Harry and Belle's home on Dayton Avenue in St. Paul. Born in Germany, Theodore came to the United States in 1914. He was 26 at the time of the census (Harry was 33), and Theodore listed his occupation as watchmaker, presumably in one of the retail jewelry stores his brothers Albert and Harry were building into a small chain. (Two other brothers, Max and Moses—sometimes called either Morris or Maurice—also came to St. Paul and entered the jewelry business).

That Harry was indeed becoming successful can be seen in the census, too. Also living in the home on Dayton Avenue was a maid; a young woman from Indiana named Francis Burrell.

Dayton Avenue is in St. Paul's Fourth Precinct. A Madison man named Jack Stevenson, 83 when interviewed for this book in 2011, knew the Goodmans in St. Paul. Stevenson, a little more than a decade younger than Bob and Irwin (Jack's older brother, Richard Stevenson, was just a year behind Bob), grew up in a house two blocks from the Goodman home on Dayton Avenue. His father was a foreman in the press room of the St. Paul Daily News and bought a diamond for Jack's mother at the Goodman Jewelers store on Seventh Street in St. Paul.

"The family was very prominent," Stevenson said of

and the Jewish Home for the Aged, 1554 Midway Parkway. Mr. Abrahamson helped organize both institutions."

Around 1880 or 1881, not long after immigrating to the United States, Louis Abrahamson married Minnie Goodman (no discernible relation to Harry J. Goodman, indeed the Prussian name of Minnie's father was spelled Gootmann, as opposed to the "Gutmann" name listed by Harry when he boarded the German ship to come to the United States in June 1899).

Louis and Minnie had their first child, a daughter, Rae Rachel, in 1882. They had nine children in all. Belle was the seventh, born October 26, 1894, in St. Paul, although some records show the birth year as 1895. One fact is not in dispute by anyone who later came to know Bob and Irwin Goodman well. Their mother—the girl, Belle, born in St. Paul just before the dawn of the 20th Century—would be the single biggest influence on the lives of Bob and Irwin.

the Goodmans. "Their uncle (Albert) had many jewelry stores. Better than 15, I think. All over Minnesota and one in La Crosse."

There is evidence that Goodman Jewelers was progressive in both its hiring practice and marketing. An item in a 1934 edition of a Twin Cities African-American publication, *The Minneapolis Spokesman*, noted that Goodman Jewelers had for 12 years at least one black employee. They also advertised in a progressive publication—progressive in that it carried news of both blacks and whites—called the *St. Paul Appeal*. A Goodman Jewelers advertisement from 1917 promoted a "jeweled Elgin watch, case guaranteed 20 years," for $9.75 or 50 cents a week. The ad calls Goodman's "the largest jeweler in the Northwest extending credit" with the flagship store at 94 East Seventh Street in St. Paul.

An ad the following year in the *Appeal* promotes an "absolutely perfect blue white diamond" for $37.50 or 50 cents a week. The 1918 ad is notable in that it includes a small photo of a man who must be either Albert or Harry Goodman, with a note that says: "Meet Goodman—Wear Diamonds." The ad promises "credit to all honest folks," and continues, quoting either Albert or Harry: "That's the way I do business. Come in and let me explain my plan. A charge account here is just the same as at any other high grade store, except you pay the amount a little each week."

By coincidence, Jack Stevenson would follow Bob and Irwin Goodman to Wisconsin after the brothers began their partnership at the jewelry store on State Street in Madison. Stevenson's father got a job at *The Capital Times* in Madison and Jack eventually re-established his friendship with Bob and Irwin. Stevenson worked as a Madison police officer and also served as county coroner. Stevenson would go to sporting events with the brothers—Jack always drove—as well as movies and restaurants. On a few occasions, Bob and Irwin would ask Stevenson to drive them back to St. Paul.

"One time in the 1980s," Stevenson said, "Bob and Irwin decided they wanted to go up to St. Paul and take a look at their old house on Dayton Avenue."

The house at 681 Dayton was still there.

"We pulled up," Stevenson recalled. "The neighborhood had changed. It was a little run down. But they got out of the car and walked up on the front porch, looked in the windows and walked around the house. I was thinking that the way the neighborhood was now, that was a good way to get shot. But nothing happened."

Stevenson said the brothers then wanted to drop in at St. Paul's St. Thomas Academy, where they had attended high school.

"It was fall and the football team was out," Stevenson said. "Bob got out of the car and walked over."

Later in life, the Goodmans' close Madison friend, Bob Pricer, asked how the brothers wound up going to a Catholic high school.

"Bob said they had a cousin who had gone to St. Thomas," Pricer said, "and his mother was not going to have a cousin get a better education than they did."

Another version of the story was that the brothers' parents thought they would be well served by the discipline inherent at a military academy like St. Thomas.

Irwin entered St. Thomas in fall 1929, after attending Marshall Junior High School. By then, according to the

Bob and Irwin's uncle, Theodore Goodman, came to the United States in 1914, and worked as a watchmaker.

Bob Goodman earned 14 varsity letters in athletics while attending St. Thomas Academy in St. Paul.

and from Fairview Avenue west to the river."

Finn worked the land, built some barns, and then, as mentioned, sold a portion of it including the buildings to Bishop Grace. Grace's intent was to "establish a school for underprivileged boys so that the pupils might learn a useful trade." The Catholic Industrial School opened in 1877 but its location was moved after only two years; in July 1884, when a new bishop, John Ireland, took over in St. Paul, he listed as a priority finding a new use for the old Finn farm and the abandoned Catholic Industrial School building.

The St. Thomas Seminary opened there Sept. 8, 1885, and was considered the umbrella organization of four schools including the College of St. Thomas and the St. Thomas Academy.

By the 1930s, when the Goodmans enrolled at St. Thomas Academy, the catalogue provided to incoming students made the St. Thomas location sound idyllic indeed, saying it "is situated near the banks of the Mississippi, in a spot of rare natural beauty, midway between the business centers of St. Paul and Minneapolis. It commands splendid vistas in every direction, and the grounds, with their groves, and undulating lawns merging in the woods and glens that border the Mississippi, form a splendid setting for an institution of learning."

From all indications, from his enrollment in 1929 onward, Irwin Goodman embraced everything St. Thomas had to offer. During his four years at the school Irwin would play in the symphonic band and be a member of both the debate club and the school yearbook—which was called *The Kaydet*—staff. In 1932 he received an Eagle Award for outstanding grades. He was a good athlete, especially in track and field, where he threw the shot-put and discus.

The 1933 *The Kaydet* summed up Irwin's years at St. Thomas with this:

"Irwin is a fine example of scholar and athlete combined. His work as an athlete in track and on the basketball floor is ample proof that he has developed body as well as mind. As a scholar he is looked up to by his classmates for his wise counsel that he is always apt to enliven with some playful joke. Precision and conscientiousness

1930 United States census, the Goodmans had moved to 902 Ashland Avenue in St. Paul. Harry listed Poland as his country of birth. Irwin was 14, Bob 10. The family had a servant living in the home, a 21 year old Minnesota native named Florence McEmery.

St. Thomas Academy dates to 1885, although the Catholic Church's ownership of what was then farmland dates to 1874, when Bishop Thomas L. Grace purchased the farm and several buildings from William Finn, an Irish immigrant who had claimed title to the land two decades earlier.

According to the 1985 book, *A Family Album: St. Thomas Academy*, by Sylvester G. Turbes, "the enterprising Finn staked out a section of land that extended roughly from what is now Marshall Avenue to St. Clair

will make him an excellent doctor someday."

There was a military presence at St. Thomas—indeed, during the years the Goodmans attended it was called the St. Thomas Military Academy, and the students were referred to as Cadets—and among the documents Irwin held on to for the remainder of his life was a certificate dated May 1933 confirming his appointment as a cadet second lieutenant.

The following fall, Irwin enrolled at the University of Minnesota while Bob followed in Irwin's footsteps at St. Thomas Academy. (Bob had attended Linwood Grade School and Maria Sanford Junior High School.) It was at St. Thomas that Bob's athleticism truly flourished. He was a four-sport star—earning 14 athletic letters—and broke the city shot put record his senior year in a meet against St. Paul Central. He was also named captain of the basketball team.

Like Irwin, Bob attained the designation of second lieutenant at St. Thomas. *The Kaydet* had this to say about Bob as he finished his time at St. Thomas:

"Athletic, military, and scholastic honors have been thoroughly tasted by Bob in his stay at St. Thomas. His most outstanding achievements, however, have been in the field of athletics, where he has excelled in football, basketball, baseball and track. Not only is he known at St. Thomas for his athletic ability, but his fame has spread throughout the Twin Cities. In the meantime, Bob's scholastic field has not been neglected, as he has earned one Eagle Award (for outstanding grades)."

At the University of Minnesota, Irwin pledged to the Phi Epsilon Pi fraternity, which nationally was founded in 1904 at City College in New York. The fraternity house in Minneapolis was located at 960 Fifteenth Avenue Southeast. Irwin eventually declared his major in business administration.

Irwin continued his accomplished track career at Minnesota, lettering his last three years. It was during his senior year in 1937 that the Gophers had a meet against the University of Wisconsin in Madison. Irwin loved what he saw of Madison—Lakes Mendota and Monona, with the downtown isthmus, home to the State Capitol building, situated between them.

It was also during that 1937 visit that Irwin dropped in on the jewelry store at 220 State Street that was owned by his father and uncles.

Goodman's Jewelers in Madison opened on June 23, 1934. A brief story in the Madison *Capital Times* newspaper a day earlier said this: "Goodman's Jewelry store will open tomorrow at 220 State Street. The new firm is owned by the Goodman brothers of St. Paul who have been active jewelers in the Middle West for the past 28 years. The store will be managed by Al Otterlee, Seattle, Wash."

Irwin Goodman competed in the discuss at the University of Minnesota, and it was on a road trip to compete against the Badgers that he fell in love with Madison.

There was a small photo of Otterlee included with the story. He looks to be about 35, neatly dressed in a coat and tie. His hair is receding above a high forehead.

It's interesting to note that at the outset, the store was given over to both jewelry and optics. A 1935 ad in the *Wisconsin State Journal* promotes "glasses—use our budget plan" and lists the store at 220 State Street as "Goodman's: Jewelers and Opticians."

By most accounts, the early years of the store in Madison were not a success. In at least one story Otterlee was

For the next 70 years – with the exception of Irwin's service in the military – the brothers would not be apart for long, and Madison would be their home.

portrayed as spending more time on the golf course than in the store. That fact was not lost on Irwin, along with his favorable impression of Madison as a whole.

Irwin graduated from the University of Minnesota in spring 1937 with a degree in business administration. His uncle Theodore gave him a car for a graduation present. Irwin went to see his father. What if he, Irwin, moved to Madison and tried his hand at the jewelry store?

Harry Gooodman thought it was a good idea, and by 1939, Irwin would be listed as owner of Goodman Jewelers on State Street in the Madison City Directory. Otterlee's name is nowhere to be seen. The manager is identified as L. V. Anderson.

Bob Goodman, meanwhile, had enrolled at the University of Minnesota. About the time Irwin was getting settled in Madison—April 1938—Bob was being initiated into the Phi Epsilon Fraternity on the Minneapolis campus.

But in September, 1939, Bob would transfer to the University of Wisconsin in Madison. For the next 70 years—with the exception of Irwin's service in the military—the brothers would not be apart for long, and Madison would be their home.

Bob later explained to *Wisconsin State Journal* sports columnist Tom Butler how it was Irwin who influenced his decision to come to Madison.

"He fell in love with Madison and urged me to join him here," Bob said. "I was attending Minnesota at that time and transferred to Wisconsin in 1939. You can't help but love this city. Madison and the university are beautiful and the people are the same."

In that same *State Journal* article (1981), Bob hinted at the close bond that developed early between the brothers and only strengthened with time. Bob told Butler that Irwin's selflessness had a major impact on how he tried to live his own life.

"I learned that from Irwin," Bob said. "If he can do something for people, he's happy. It's a way of life with him. I was more rough and tough, but when you're around Irwin a lot, you learn how to treat people nicely."

Bob would eventually earn a bachelor of philosophy degree in economics at UW–Madison, and, of course, he played sports.

The November 19, 1939, issue of the *B'Nai B'rith Hillel Review*—published on the Madison campus by the foundation of the same name—noted that Bob had been a welcome addition to the Phi Epsilon fraternity football team.

"At fullback and utility there is Bob Goodman," the paper wrote. "Goodman made his impression from the start with his accurate passing. It was an offense built around Goodman that made the Phi Eps a team to contend with. Opponents had nothing but superlatives for his accurate passing."

By the following year, 1940, the same publication was writing Bob up for his softball exploits. The May 23 edition listed the campus "All Star Jewish Softball Team" with Bob Goodman as first-team pitcher.

By that time—1940—Bob and Irwin were, of course, living in Madison.

The 1939 Madison city directory showed Irwin as living at 1114 Spaight Street. The St. Paul city directory of that same year showed Bob living with his parents, Harry and Belle, at 1074 Goodrich Avenue. By September of that year, Bob would be down in Madison enrolled at the University of Wisconsin.

Meanwhile, Irwin had purchased the State Street jewelry store from his father and uncle. Business had not been good at the store compared to other Goodman properties and Irwin was determined to turn it around. It was not, from the outset, a simple endeavor.

"It was hard going at first," Bob Pricer said. Irwin had shared stories of those early days. Pricer said, "Irwin would talk about how days would go by without a customer."

Matters weren't helped when the city of Madison decided in the spring of 1939 to repave and improve State Street, including the installation of curb and gutter. (In the 1970s State Street would become a pedestrian mall open only to city buses, but for decades prior it was busy with cars and one of Madison's most popular retail shopping destinations).

Among the other retailers besides Goodman Jewelers on State Street in spring 1939 were Brown's Book Shop; the Campus Record Shop; a market, the Triangle Food Shop; Capital City Rent-a-Car; Madison Photo; Karl Theis Shoe Repair; the William Busch Beauty Salon; several clothing stores—Tiffany's, Lefco's, Two Millers, Wagner's and Jack & Jill, the latter a kids' store; and even another jeweler, L. Wuilleumier, in the 400 block of State.

A couple dozen of the State Street retailers got together on May 16, 1939 and took out a full-page ad in *The Capital Times* encouraging their customers to brave the construction.

"This is Tough on Both of Us," the advertisement read. "BUT IT'S WORTH IT!" It continued, "Maybe it's costing you a moment's extra time to get down State Street, but these merchants make it worth your while. When this job is done—and it's going to be worth it— State Street will be the foremost thoroughfare in Madison. We urge you to come down and shop with us and watch the big steam shovel work."

In early July, with the street repair finished, Irwin suffered another setback. The jewelry store at 220 State Street was adjacent to—and actually shared the main floor of the Weber Building at 218-220 State Street—with the Weber Restaurant, which opened in 1924. The building had apartments on the second and third floors.

At 3 a.m. on July 6, 1939, a fire started in the basement of the Weber Restaurant. It spread quickly to the restaurant proper, as well as the upstairs apartments. It was a serious fire, and while all residents of the apart-

From left, Irwin, Belle, Harry and Bob Goodman. Once Harry and Belle moved to Madison, the family lived together in an elegant apartment on East Gilman Street.

Bob Goodman was a highly accomplished baseball and softball player during his early Madison years, and eventually was inducted into the Madison Sports Hall of Fame.

The article continued, with a mention of Irwin Goodman:

"Apartment dwellers sat on the recently constructed State Street curb most of the night while firemen fought the blaze. The second floor apartments were damaged considerably by water and smoke, while the fire burned through a center wall. The third floor, however, suffered little with the exception of the smoke.

The Goodman jewelry store, which shares the main floor of the Weber building with the restaurant, was damaged by smoke, water and burning within the center wall.

Irwin Goodman, proprietor of the jewelry store, said he was unable to estimate the damage, but reported his stock was insured."

Thirteen months after the fire, in August 1940, it was Irwin himself, and not the store, sustaining the damage. Irwin fractured an ankle playing softball. At 25, he was already well known enough around Madison that his injury made page two of *The Capital Times*.

"Irwin Goodman Breaks Ankle in Ball Game" read the headline, and the story noted he was taken to Madison General Hospital for treatment.

According to an interview Bob Goodman later gave to Tom Butler of the *Wisconsin State Journal*, Irwin's injury was responsible for Bob—who had played baseball during his time at the University of Minnesota—not playing varsity baseball at Wisconsin.

"Bob had to help with the business," Butler wrote.

When Irwin sustained his injury he was playing for the YMCA softball team. Both Irwin and Bob got involved with the YMCA around 1940. This early entry into the world of service organizations would not surprise anyone who knew the Goodmans later, when such groups, particularly Rotary, were an integral part of their lives.

In January 1941 Bob and Irwin were both founding members of a club supplemental to the YMCA that would focus on public speaking and training for administrating public meetings and programs.

By that year, 1941, Bob and Irwin's parents, Harry and Belle Goodman, had moved to Madison.

ments were able to escape safely outside, four Madison firefighters suffered injuries battling the blaze.

A *Capital Times* account noted:

"Escaping refrigerator gas in the basement of the restaurant temporarily blinded two firemen while another was completely overcome. A falling coffee cooker slightly injured another. Firemen had to break through a wall of Goodman Jewelers to fight the blaze."

Bob and Irwin moved with Harry and Belle into an elegant apartment at 1 East Gilman Street, an apartment building that had once housed the Quisling Medical Clinic and was known as the Quisling Towers.

Ghita Bessman became a good friend of Bob and Irwin, and she first met them around 1950 when she and her husband, Leonard Bessman—an attorney and, later, federal bankruptcy judge—had an apartment in the building at 1 East Gilman.

"They were on top, in the penthouse," Ghita recalled of the Goodmans.

Her first impression of Bob and Irwin? "My first impression was that they were tall," she said. "They were very sweet and had nice things to say about everybody. I think people wondered about that. How can they say such nice things about everybody? Some might have thought it was insincere. I'm confident it was sincere."

Another longtime friend, Joe Silverberg, first met the Goodmans when they lived in an apartment at 1 East Gilman Street. His mother, Rose, and Belle Goodman were good friends.

"They lived very graciously," Silverberg recalled of the Goodmans in the 1940s. "They had the best apartment in the Quisling Towers. The top apartment. It had two floors and faced due west."

Both Ghita Bessman and Joe Silverberg remember two things about the Goodmans in their early Madison years: the brothers' devotion to one another, and to their mother.

Ghita called the relationship between Bob and Irwin "quite remarkable. I don't know that they ever had a rough word with one another. Irwin must have heard Bob's jokes a thousand times, but he'd smile and say, 'Oh, Bob.' And Bob thought Irwin was the greatest. They were both right."

Joe Silverberg recalls Belle Goodman as "a very vivacious woman," and Ghita concurs. "She was a lovely woman," Ghita said. Belle also set an example for her sons in her efforts to help the less fortunate.

Ghita recalled, "She would go to visit people who were ill, and needed attention of some kind. Bob and Irwin were impressed by that, and of course they followed in those footsteps."

In 2003, *Connections*—the newsletter of Jewish Social Services in Madison—published an article in tribute to Belle Goodman in which a number of people, including Joe Silverberg, offered their recollections of Belle.

A lifelong Madisonian named Anita Parks said, "Everyone thought she was the most gorgeous, elegant lady in the world. Belle was a role model, not only for her sons, but for all the women in the community. She set the example and is responsible for what her sons are today."

On a less serious note, Anita Parks added, "Mrs.

> *Belle was a role model, not only for her sons, but for all the women in the community. She set the example and is responsible for what her sons are today.*

Goodman made the world's greatest apple pie out of Ritz crackers."

The 2003 *Connections* piece also quoted Ida Swarsensky, widow of Rabbi Manfred Swarsensky, who founded Temple Beth El in Madison.

Mrs. Swarsensky said she "never heard a negative word about Belle Goodman," adding that Belle was "a real lady." Of particular note was Belle's volunteer work that included visiting disadvantaged children. After those visits, Belle made a point of remembering the kids' birthdays.

Shirley Sweet, Temple Beth El secretary, recalled Belle as "very philanthropic" and "a woman who joined every service organization."

That seemed a fair statement. Among the groups Belle Goodman belonged to were the United Givers Association; the Council of Jewish Women; the Eastern Star; Temple Beth El Sisterhood; and the Madison Jewish Welfare Council.

The *Connections* piece concluded with this tribute to Belle Goodman: "Thanks for the charitable acts, the mitzvot that you performed in your own right. But, thanks also for raising two menschen, two quality human beings

Irwin said his years spent serving in the United States Army, his first great adventure away from home, were among the happiest of his life.

with such and abiding sense of tzedakah, righteousness, that they have provided the Jewish community and Dane County with two lifetimes filled with countless acts of immeasurable generosity."

By the end of 1941, with Belle and Harry in Madison, Irwin was recovered from his broken ankle and Bob, who was still in school at UW–Madison, could once again think about sports. That Irwin was back in charge of Goodman's Jewelry Store was evident by a full page newspaper advertisement in *The Capital Times* on Dec. 31, 1941. "These Madison Business and Professional Men Wish You a Happy New Year," the ad read, and pictured were no less than 42 movers and shakers from the Madison community. Irwin, his photo between a clothier and a banker, appears to be one of the youngest pictured.

Bob, while certainly helping in the business, also dedicated himself to athletics, especially softball. Bob first played on the YMCA team—the same squad Irwin was on when he broke his ankle—but Bob wasn't on Madison diamonds long before Ray Sennett, a softball pioneer and eventual member of the Madison Sports Hall of Fame, recruited him to play for the team sponsored by Security State Bank, a top team in the Major Softball League, Madison's best.

"Bob could have been a professional baseball player," said Jack Stevenson, who had known the Goodmans since their St. Paul days and moved to Madison after they did. Stevenson recalled going to softball games with his parents and said Bob Goodman was the star player on Security State Bank, which had a roster full of good players. (Bob also played for Security's team in the city basketball league.)

He was best at softball and baseball. In June 1942, shortly after graduating from the University of Wisconsin, Bob got a headline in the *Wisconsin State Journal* when he broke up the opposing pitcher's no-hitter in the 12th inning, driving in two runs and clinching a 2-1 softball victory for Security State Bank over Frankie's Tavern.

"The win was the 13th straight for the unbeaten Bankers," the story noted, "who had already clinched the first round championship two nights ago."

With two on and two out in the bottom of the 12th, and after Frankie's had scored in the top of the 12th to go up 1-0, Bob looped a soft single over the third baseman's head, allowing the tying and winning runs to score.

That game was played at Franklin Field—later Goodman Park, after the gift from Bob and Irwin that included the city's first municipal swimming pool—but part of Bob's athletic legacy in Madison was accomplished playing hardball at a classic old stadium on East Washington Avenue named Breese Stevens Field.

Breese Stevens had hosted legends, including the eventual Heisman Trophy winner Alan Ameche when Ameche was still a high school football star in Kenosha. Tom Butler would recall in the *State Journal* that at Breese Stevens Ameche "ran with the ferocity of a wild stallion." Butler also remembered seeing the great Jesse Owens race a thoroughbred horse around the track at Breese Stevens.

As Butler noted, Breese Stevens was where Madison's Industrial Baseball League—a hardball league—played its games. Butler waxed almost poetic, with a nod to Bob Goodman, recalling those glory days:

"That's where guys like Bob King, Gene Calhoun, Otto Puls, Knobby Kelliher, Bob Goodman and a host of other outstanding ballplayers avoided a misspent youth by trodding that hallowed ground with regularity each summer." The Industrial Baseball League teams Bob played on included those sponsored by the West Side Businessmen, Bowman Dairy and Gardner Bakery.

Capital Times sports editor Art Hinrichs, who pitched in the Industrial League, recalled Bob hitting one of the longest home runs ever seen at Breese Stevens Field. It may have stuck in Hinrichs' memory—the fans went crazy, he said—because it was Hinrichs himself who offered up what he called a "gopher ball" that Bob blasted high over the right center field fence.

Still, it was softball where Bob really made his name in Madison amateur sports. He played 12 years for Security State Bank, starting in the early 1940s, and in seven of those years the team won the city championship. Decades later, recalling that dominant run, Security manager Joe Kocvara called Bob the Bankers' "all time best hitter."

He was also a good outfielder. In 1948, Bob led a team of Major League all-stars against a similar team from Milwaukee in a game played at Breese Stevens Field. Butler wrote, "Bob preserved a 4-1 victory with three outstanding defensive plays, including a catch of what almost certainly would have been a home run."

The 1949 and 1950 seasons may have been the zenith for both Bob and his Security State Bank team. Across those two seasons the Bankers won 62 games and lost 19. In 1949, Bob batted .348, second on the team, and led the club with five home runs.

The front page of the *Wisconsin State Journal* sports section of August 29, 1949, is dominated by a photograph headlined: "Captured Madison's 1949 Major Softball Championship." The Security State Bank team is pictured, and the cutline explains they beat Frankie's Tavern 7-0 for the title. Bob Goodman is standing in the middle of the back row, with a tanned face and a smile that reaches his eyes.

The following year, 1950, Bob hit .352 to lead the Bankers, and also contributed a team high seven doubles and four home runs.

Later in life, Bob would tell stories about those heady days, but he was more given to humor than detailing his own exploits. He recalled having the occasional run-in with umpires, including one that pitted him against the veteran ump Sam Dixon.

"He called a strike on me once that I said was a ball," Bob told Tom Butler years later. "The next pitch came in the same place and he called strike while I argued ball. He finally said to me, 'One more ball like that and you're out.'"

If Bob could entertain later in life with stories from the baseball and softball diamond, his older brother had tales from his years in the United States Army. Irwin served from 1943 to 1945 and decades later told a good friend that the years were among the happiest of his life.

That may appear unusual on the surface, but it seems fair to speculate that Irwin's time in the service was his first great adventure away from home. After all, not long after his move to Madison, he was joined by his brother, and soon, his parents. When Irwin was inducted into the Army on January 5, 1943, he was on his own.

A *Wisconsin State Journal* story published when Irwin completed his service noted that he finished "basic training at Fort Warren, Wyoming, and later served for a year and a half as special services officer at the army service forces training center at Camp Lee, Virginia. In that capacity he directed the sports and recreation program of the center as well as handling war bond sales and insurance matters, for which he received a certificate of commendation from the commanding general."

Irwin was discharged from the Army at Fort Meade, Maryland in late 1945, and returned to Madison.

In short order his focus would return to the State Street jewelry store that had now been under his ownership for nearly a decade. Irwin, with help from Bob, was ready to take a good store and make it great.

CHAPTER 3
Jewel of State Street

But the decade of the 1950s began on a sad note—the death, on September 25, 1950, of Harry J. Goodman.

It was front page news that afternoon in Madison's *Capital Times* newspaper. Under a photo of Harry that showed him with a small smile, rimless glasses, a fedora and crisply knotted necktie, the headline read: "H. J. Goodman Dies, Age 70; Jeweler Here." The story began:

"Harry J. Goodman, 70, for many years associated with Goodman's jewelry store at 220 State Street, died today at a local hospital after a long illness. He resided at 1 E. Gilman Street.

Mr. Goodman had been a Madison resident since 1940, moving here from St. Paul.

Survivors include his wife, two sons, Irwin and Robert, at home, and two brothers, Theodore and Morris, St. Paul."

Harry Goodman's funeral was three days later, September 28, 1950, a Thursday, at the Frautschi funeral home in Madison. The officiating rabbi was Manfred Swarsensky, who, like Harry, emigrated to the United States from eastern Europe. Swarsensky had been a rabbi in Berlin and survived several months in a concentration camp in Sachsenhausen, until one day in 1939 when he was unexpectedly set free on the condition he leave Germany. Swarsensky landed in Chicago after brief stays in Holland and England, and came to Madison in 1940, accepting a position at the new Temple Beth El.

The Swarsensky name, like the Goodman name, would come to be revered in Madison. The rabbi fought discrimination and was renowned for building bridges between opposing factions on a wide variety of issues. When Swarsensky died, in 1981, Madison's Downtown Rotary established The Manfred F. Swarsensky Humanitarian Service Award to honor individuals who display through their voluntary efforts the spirit Swarsensky exhibited in his lifetime. Harry Goodman's sons, Bob and Irwin, were both recipients of the Swarsensky Award.

Of course, that was far in the future in September 1950, when Swarsensky officiated at Harry Goodman's funeral. Burial was in the Forest Hill cemetery in Madison and the pallbearers were Joseph Rothschild, S.L. Goldstine, J.J. Sinagub, I.J. Gold, Albert Dizon, Louis Paley, Jerome J. Sinaiko, A. J. Sweet, Julius Ciller, Dr. Chester Kurtz, Dr. Herman Shapiro, F.R. Conner, Sol Frank, and Everett Sloggett.

It is said that the death of one's father is a time of

From left, Irwin, Harry and Bob Goodman. Harry died in 1950, and is buried in Madison's Forest Hill cemetery.

the Goodman jewelry stores throughout the Midwest were a considerable part of his legacy. As Harry said—and their mother Belle reiterated—success allowed you to give back to the community that helped make you successful, and nothing was more important than that.

To be successful in the jewelry business, Bob and Irwin had a few core principles, including establishing solid relationships with vendors and always having a good mix of inventory, sold at a fair price. But really, what drove their success was the belief—really an extension of their personalities and values—that their employees were family and their customers an extension of that family.

"It was like a family," said John Hayes of the relationship between Bob and Irwin and their employees. Hayes worked for the Goodmans for many years before eventually buying the store from them.

Hayes started with the Goodmans in 1983 and nearly three decades later was still hearing stories from former longtime employees about how they were treated by the brothers.

"One of the fellows who was here when I started was a man named Henry Rahn," Hayes said. "Just recently his son brought me in some photos of holiday parties that Henry and his wife hosted. They were family parties, but Bob and Irv were there. The people who worked for them were a big part of their lives outside the store as well."

Hayes learned quickly that Goodman employees tended to stay Goodman employees.

"When I started, the watchmaker had just retired after being there 30 years," Hayes said. "Their store manager, Hy Grossman, had recently retired—he'd been there about 25 years. Judy Schenk, who took over as store manager when I got there, had 25 years in and stayed another 10 after I got there."

Hayes continued, "They were ahead of the curve as far as taking care of their employees. They set up a profit sharing and pension plan and funded it completely. When people retired, they were able to retire comfortably. That was ahead of its time. Their philosophy of philanthropy extended to caring for their own employees. It was pretty cool."

The Goodmans in turn expected their staff to go the

reckoning for any man. Thoughts of one's own mortality are inescapable. Still, it would be a decade or longer before Irwin Goodman, and to a lesser extent his brother Bob, embraced a strict health-centered lifestyle in the belief it might allow them a longer life than their father. In the immediate aftermath of Harry's death in 1950, it may be that the brothers felt compelled to give greater attention to their jewelry business. Though their father had not been actively involved in the State Street store,

extra mile for every customer who came in the store, and to that end, they led by example.

"Bob knew the name of every customer who walked in the store," said Arlon Mason, a longtime jewelry wholesaler in Madison who began calling on the Goodmans in the 1970s and subsequently became a good friend, close enough that Bob and Irwin sponsored his application to the Madison Downtown Rotary.

"Bob had a stool," Mason continued. "It was like a bar stool, placed at the back of the store, and Bob would sit on that stool and greet every person who came into Goodman's. It didn't matter who they were or what they were there for. Sometimes it was just to make a payment of a couple of dollars. There was a teller's window inside where people could come and make a payment."

Mason was impressed early by both the level of service and also how Bob, always affable, nevertheless managed to always know whatever was happening in the store.

"They had a sales clerk for every case in that store," Mason said. "A case is only six feet long. The amount of service they provided was nothing short of spectacular. You could not walk in the store and get 'no' for an answer. That's probably their claim to fame. If Bob heard one of the sales people saying no—at any point in the conversation, for any reason—that meant they had to go back into the office and have a conversation with Bob. They all learned quickly that they could say anything in the world they wanted, except they could not say no. Bob's mantra was we will do whatever the customer wants. The level of service from Goodman Jewelers—when Bob was in the store especially—was like nothing I had ever seen."

That point was echoed by one longtime Goodman customer, Paul Reilly, who spent many years as the comptroller for the city of Madison.

"Bob was absolutely incredible," Reilly said. "A master salesman."

Reilly recalled once being in Goodman's trying to buy his wife, Barb, an emerald ring. He had done some research and had a pretty good idea of what he wanted, and what the salesman was showing that day wasn't it.

"Each gem had a little imperfection," Reilly said.

Bob, left, worked the "front of the house" at the jewelry story, while Irwin, who kept the books, worked the back.

Suddenly, Bob Goodman appeared at the shoulder of the salesman. "He must have overheard," Reilly said.

As Reilly recalled, Bob said, "I have some emeralds arriving in a week or so. You might like one of those better."

"Sure enough," Reilly said, "10 days later I walked in the store and Bob pulled out an envelope with eight or nine emeralds. One of them was just right. He really zeroed in on what the customer wanted, and what the customer could afford."

Barb Reilly was Barb Braeger and not yet married when she first went to Goodman's.

"My mother shopped there," Barb recalled.

When Barb graduated from Madison Central High School in 1955, she became a Goodman's customer herself. The Goodmans gave a sterling silver demitasse spoon to every female Central graduate. It was a nice gesture but also brilliant from a business standpoint: exposing the young

Early on, the Goodmans sponsored an annual bowling contest for men and women that awarded the winners a dress-style watch.

women to Goodman's just as they are poised to begin earning money and presumably become more sophisticated about jewelry. Barb herself became a customer almost as soon as she received her free spoon, buying a set of silver plates that she paid for at the rate of $1 a week.

Arlon Mason, the wholesaler, noted, "The business, real quick, became about people getting married."

The Goodmans paid attention to local high school graduations, and, of course, they were close to the University of Wisconsin—both physically close on State Street and emotionally close as athletic boosters—with its wealth of young people reaching marriage age.

"It wasn't unusual," Mason said, "for a Goodman's customer to come to buy an engagement ring for their fiancée, and before they were done, Bob would have helped them arrange a limousine for the big night, a restaurant reservation, everything so the proposal and the presentation of the ring went off perfectly. Because they were buying the ring from him."

Mason continued, "Wedding and engagement rings became the anchors of their business. Goodman Jewelers

was, and is, the bridal destination. The thing is, if they buy the wedding ring from your store, the rest of their lives, if they need a piece of jewelry, they're going to come to your store."

Longtime employee and current Goodman's owner John Hayes concurs.

"Bridal has always been a mainstay," he said. "A big, important part of the business. Engagement and wedding rings. Part of that is setting up a relationship with the customer. Bob always said that one sale will not make you rich or poor. It's the long term relationships that you build with people that's going to make you successful."

Hayes felt the Bob and Irwin's willingness to allow people to make time payments also strengthened the bond with their clientele.

"They did a lot of business on credit without requiring interest or carrying charges," Hayes said. "They would work with people to make it easier for them to get something really special."

Part of it was that the Goodmans, especially Bob, really did enjoy meeting people, chatting, trading a joke, and, in the case of an attractive woman, maybe even becoming a little flirtatious.

"Bob was a flirt," Barb Reilly recalled fondly. "First with my mom and then with me."

This was echoed by another Goodman customer, Dolores Tollefson, who in 1948, out of high school and just 17 years old, got a job with the telephone company in downtown Madison.

"I needed a wristwatch," Dolores recalled, some 65 years later. "So I went to Goodman's." Dolores was earning $8 a week and the watch she wanted was a Bulova that cost $35. Bob was assisting her.

"I haven't got that much money," she said.

"I'll give you a charge account," Bob said.

They arranged two payments of $17.50 each.

"My first charge account," Dolores said.

Of Bob, she recalled, "He was a real nice guy." But she was cautious a few years later, after she had moved into an apartment at 321 Wisconsin Avenue, not far from where the Goodmans lived at 1 E. Gilman.

In the evening, after work—this was in 1953—

Dolores, who lived on the third floor, would sit in a swing on the front porch. Most nights Bob Goodman would stroll by on his own way home from work. Presumably he recognized Dolores—Bob had an encyclopedic memory for names and faces—and one evening he stopped as he walked past.

"Would you have dinner with me?" Bob said.

"Oh, thank you, but I don't think so," Dolores said.

The next night, Bob asked again. Dolores declined. Bob said, "If you'll come, I'll give you something nice from the store."

Recalling the moment decades later, Dolores chuckled. "I figured I knew what he wanted for dessert!" So they never did have that dinner. Her sister later chastised her for not going and Dolores herself wondered how it would have gone.

Tom Grannis was not a Goodman's customer when he first came to Madison, in 1956. Grannis was with the Air Force and had come to Madison to be stationed at Truax Field. One day the Air Force did some drills up and down State Street. That's when Grannis saw the store.

"They had quality control standards that were so tight, they might reject 70 percent of the merchandise that came into the store," Mason said.

"If I ever need a jewelry store," Grannis said to himself, "that's where I'll go."

Two years later, in 1958, he needed a wristwatch, and he went to Goodman's. He introduced himself to Bob, who sold him a watch with part of the money down, the rest made in time payments. A year later, Grannis bought his wife's wedding ring from Bob.

But it was a decade later when Grannis had an experience with the Goodmans that he never forgot, even a half century later. Grannis was going to MATC on the GI Bill, and the first day of school, he learned students were expected to buy textbooks at the conclusion of each class. He hadn't brought sufficient cash. Grannis remembered

that the Goodman Jewelry store was just across the Capitol Square from MATC. At lunch hour, he walked across the Square to State Street, and into the store, where he found Bob Goodman.

"I have a problem," Grannis said, and explained the situation.

"How much do you need?" Bob said.

"One hundred dollars," Grannis said.

Bob went into the back of the store and came out with $100 in cash.

"Do you want me to sign anything?" Grannis asked.

"Of course not," Bob said. "I know you."

The next day, Grannis repaid the loan. "A handshake was all we ever needed," Grannis said.

His daughter's husband bought their wedding ring from Goodman's, and Tom's son did, too. Of Irwin and Bob, Grannis said, "They were men of character."

According to wholesaler Arlon Mason, they also really knew their business.

"They had quality control standards that were so tight, they might reject 70 percent of the merchandise that came into the store," Mason said. "They shipped it back. It didn't meet the Goodman standard. It drove the manufacturers crazy." Mason continued, "Bob would take a tweezers and squeeze the diamonds. If one was solid, but not really solid, it could crack. Bob would send it back to the manufacturer. They did that with every piece, but especially diamonds. The business is all about selling diamonds. That's where the money is."

According to Mason, the Goodmans hired knowledgeable employees, and a lot of them.

"They had more watchmakers and gemologists than anyone in the state."

In the late 1950s, the Goodmans expanded their watch repair department, and used the occasion to promote a lengthy feature article in the *Wisconsin State Journal*.

"They were masters of publicity," Mason said.

The article, which appeared in the *State Journal* in August 1960, profiled three Goodman's watchmakers. It focused on innovations in the watch-making craft. The article said such mechanical aids—ultrasonic cleaning equipment, precision micrometers, and something called

The Goodmans were avid supporters of University of Wisconsin athletics, and often provided watches that served as prizes at season-ending awards banquets.

a "cardiograph" to check the most expensive timepieces—were really only truly effective ". . . if they're in the hands of individuals bettering themselves at their exacting life work."

The article then introduced the "Goodman team" of watchmakers. Jan C. Vander Way, a native of Holland, who lived through the Nazi occupation, attended a watchmaking trade school in his country and then emigrated to Illinois, joining the Goodmans in November 1959. James Witzke joined Goodman's in the same month, the time of the watch repair expansion, having attended a watch making school in Denver. He worked at jewelry stores in Oshkosh and Green Bay before coming to Madison. The watch repair department was run by Francis Kress, who had been at the store since 1953.

It was extraordinary publicity for a retail jeweler, but it was not unusual for the Goodmans where the Madison media was concerned. For most years in the 1960s, when Irwin would make a buying trip abroad, he would return with a photo of himself examining diamonds in some distant port, and that photo would appear in the Madison papers.

"The trips were as much about publicity as anything else," Arlon Mason said. "Most of the manufacturers would have come to them, and did."

In June 1961 a boxed photograph with a lengthy caption appeared in *The Capital Times* under the headline, "Examining Diamonds." The photo showed Irwin and a representative of a Holland diamond firm looking at stones in Amsterdam. The caption read, "They are examining diamonds which Goodman purchased for Goodman Jewelers here for sale in the fall. Goodman said that by buying diamonds in Amsterdam, or Antwerp, the Holland diamond centers, jewelers may offer a price break to their customers."

Four summers later, in July 1965, Irwin was again pictured in *The Capital Times*, with another extended caption below the headline, "Diamond Process." Irwin was standing at the shoulder of a seated woman who was working on a diamond. The caption read, "Irwin Goodman of Madison's Goodman Jewelers observes one of the diamond cutting and polishing processes in one of the world's leading diamond centers, Antwerp, Belgium. Goodman recently returned from one of his annual trips to Antwerp for purchase of diamonds for sale by his firm in Madison. The worker here is engaged in girdling, which is the first stage of the diamond cutting process."

In May 1960, the photo was of a woman, Irene Duma of Madison, and it appeared in a column in *The Capital Times* called "The Feminine Angle." The item reported that Irene was wearing a most unusual bauble: "The largest cultured pearl in the world, named the Miracle of the Sea, formerly owned by the Empress Dowager of China and valued at more than $100,000, is on display this week as part of the new connoisseur collection of Imperial cultured pearls at Goodman Jewelers."

At other times Irwin's trips generated not just photos and captions but lengthy news stories. In November 1962 the *Wisconsin State Journal* ran a long piece detailing Irwin's visit to Belgium, noting that he stayed in Brussels but made a daily commute to Antwerp, where he would meet with brokers.

The story, written by James Burgess, who would later become publisher of the *State Journal*, noted that the 1962 trip was Irwin's fourth to Belgium. He told Burgess he spent 10 days looking at diamonds in the offices of brokers and purchased nearly 1,000 diamonds, which, because of the time of clearing customs, were shipped to Madison in small parcels after Irwin's return. "Some will be mounted in pins and settings, some are center stones for rings," Burgess wrote.

Just over a year later, in December 1963, there was an-

other prominently placed news story and photo, this time in *The Capital Times*, under the headline: "Despite High Sums, Diamond Business Relies on Trust." The secondary headline spoke to the Goodmans' ability to generate news coverage, and might have given their competitors pause. It simply read: "Goodman Reports on Buying Trip."

The story described how Irwin had just returned from a trip in which, again, he had "selected nearly 1,000 diamonds."

> ## *"The Goodman brothers – Bob and Irwin – will never win Emmys for their TV performances," Carr wrote.*

The Capital Times story got a little more in depth on Irwin's relationship with diamond brokers. It began, "The diamond marketing business is one of the most unusual in the world because, in spite of high sums involved, it is done 'on trust' among the brokers, Irwin A. Goodman, who recently returned from a diamond buying trip to Antwerp, Belgium, said today."

Irwin was quoted: "A written contract is about unknown in the diamond business."

The accompanying photo showed Irwin at a "diamond manufacturing establishment" in Antwerp. The balance of the story explained—with further quotes from Irwin—the role of brokers in the diamond business.

By 1970, Irwin was still generating news coverage for his trips. In June of that year, on the front of its business section the *Wisconsin State Journal* pictured Irwin smiling and holding a large diamond between the thumb and forefinger of his right hand.

The extended cutline read, "Big enough to catch Elizabeth Taylor's eye, this 12 carat, pear-shaped diamond was one of thousands that Irwin Goodman looked at during a recent buying trip to Antwerp, Belgium.

"Goodman, of Goodman's Jewelers, 220 State St., goes at least once a year to Antwerp, 'the oldest market in the world for diamonds.'"

"Antwerp has been a diamond center for probably 500 years, he said. The diamonds come from African mines and are cut and polished in European factories. Diamond brokers sell them to jewelers like Goodman and their buyers.

"Many people are investing in diamonds today, buying the stones and holding them in bank vaults, waiting for their value to appreciate, Goodman said."

One of the final accounts of Irwin's buying trips came in the *Wisconsin State Journal* in 1973, and it was a trip not to Belgium but instead to the Premier Diamond Mine in Pretoria, South Africa.

Crowds of up to 15,000 packed the University of Wisconsin Field House for boxing matches, and Bob and Irwin were among the most enthusiastic fans.

"I knew they didn't just pick diamonds off the ground," Irwin told writer Bill Wineke. "But it is an impressive process to watch the men separate a diamond from 6,150 pounds of ore."

Irwin explained that the process as he had viewed it is arduous, with each diamond being extracted on average from stone 14 million times its weight.

"They showed me the results of a previous day's mining," Irwin said, "and, when you see a whole day's recovery sitting in a little box, it doesn't seem like an awful lot."

Bob and Irwin parlayed the extraordinary news coverage of their business with advertising and promotions that kept the store and the Goodman name in front of the public.

In 1951, the Goodmans began a lengthy association with WMTV in Madison, which was then Channel 33. (In 1960, the station became Channel 15.) The most memorable television spots probably involved Bob appearing on camera himself, occasionally singing "diamonds are a girl's best friend."

Irwin also appeared in some spots, and the commercials featuring the brothers in one way or another endured across three decades.

In 1984, Debra Carr began a *Capital Times* story on a number of local businessmen featuring themselves in television ads by focusing on the Goodmans.

"They stand stiffly behind the jewelry counter," Carr wrote in her lead. "Staring into the camera with frozen smiles, they invite television viewers 'to visit the diamond store of Madison.'

"The Goodman brothers—Bob and Irwin—will never win Emmys for their TV performances," Carr continued. "But they're among many local business proprietors who star in their own ads."

Bob was quoted: "Lots of people have grown up seeing us on TV. I used to sing the jingle 'diamonds are a girl's best friend.' I know that I don't have a great voice and people would kid me about my singing, but it helped to develop a rapport with customers and friends."

When they weren't promoting one specific item or another at the store in a TV spot, Bob would sometimes appear to introduce a program sponsored by the Goodmans.

A newspaper ad in 1953 in the *Wisconsin State Journal* touted a movie, "National Honeymoon," starring Diana Lynn and Dick Haymes, which was appearing at 9 p.m. that night on "Goodman Jewelers' All-Star Hollywood Theater."

More than two decades on, a similar newspaper ad invited readers to watch the police show, "Adam-12," presented by Goodman's Jewelers, "the diamond store of Madison." The copy read, "Irwin and Bob Goodman invite you to watch "Adam-12" in action every Thursday night.

"They did things in advertising that were years ahead of everybody else," Arlon Mason said. Often they involved promotions or cooperative advertising with a major jewelry wholesaler. Mason was working for Seiko in the 1970s and recalled how the company had struggled to crack the graduation market for watches. He brought it up to Bob Goodman.

"Bob suggested we run some ads during the WIAA Boys Basketball Tournament, which was televised statewide," Mason said. "Bob knew all the guys at Channel 27 in Madison, which was the flagship station for the tournament. It was very popular and hard to buy time."

But because the Goodmans were involved, Mason

said, Channel 27 met with him and wound up outlining an extensive buy that would put Seiko front and center during the tournament and would cost $78,000.

Mason said, "The Seiko vice-president drove up from Chicago with a check. The Goodmans picked up half of it. The ad said you could get Seiko watches at Goodman's Jewelers."

Other promotions involved other jewelry firms. When, in 1956, Feature Ring Co. sponsored a "Queen of Diamonds" contest nationally, Goodman's got involved and encouraged their customers to fill out entries. A Madison woman, Clara Stude, took second place and won $500 cash and $750 worth of diamonds. Bob and Irwin were pictured in the news story handing her a check.

The same year Goodman's Jewelers began advertising on WMTV, 1951, they launched a bowling contest that endured for decades. In association with Elgin watches, Goodman's presented both the male and female bowlers scoring the highest "triplicate" score made during the city league season with an Elgin watch. The male winner got a water- and shock-proof watch while the female winner received a 17-jewel Elgin dress style watch.

A "triplicate" is the same score rolled in three consecutive games and Bob later explained how he, Irwin, and *Capital Times* bowling writer Art Hinrichs had come up with it as a way to allow even average bowlers a chance to win the prize. For instance, one year, three games of 158 in the same series were high.

"There are so many average bowlers out there and they never get an award," Bob said. "Everybody can't always be a winner, but it's nice they can be recognized."

Bob's comments were made to *The Capital Times* in the fall of 1987 as their "triplicate" contest began its 37th year.

"We enjoy people and that's why we do it," Bob said. "It gives every man and woman, young and old, a chance to win."

The Goodmans also teamed with Elgin to honor the elite in one of the brothers' favorite sports, college boxing. Many people today have either forgotten or never knew what a major sport varsity boxing was at UW–Madison. Nowhere was college boxing bigger. Crowds of up to 15,000 packed the University of Wisconsin Field House

for home matches, and Bob and Irwin were among the most enthusiastic fans. I know, because Bob told me. He called me at my newspaper office after I wrote a book on the rise and fall of college boxing in Madison—the sport ended here, and nationally, when a Badger boxer died following his NCAA championship bout in the Field House.

That tragedy happened in April, 1960. The mood was much more upbeat in spring 1956 when the Goodmans attended the annual banquet for the boxing team which that year was held at the Elks Club in downtown Madison. The team was one of the most outstanding in the long tenure of revered Badger boxing coach John Walsh. One of the highlights of the banquet was the presentation by Bob and Irwin of specially designed Elgin watches to six Badger boxers. (Later, when the football Badgers went to the Rose Bowl in 1963, the entire team received Elgin 30-jewel watches from the Goodmans that were presented on the Christmas Eve prior to the New Year's Day game.) In 1956, the watches in boxing were awarded to the five Badgers who won individual NCAA championships. The sixth watch, the Goodmans said at the banquet, was for team captain Ev Chambers, who, while he did not win a title, surely deserved it for providing the leadership that produced such an extraordinary season. It was the Badgers' eighth, and last, national championship.

Bob and Irwin would occasionally go to Chicago for professional bouts as well. Roundy Coughlin, the *Wisconsin State Journal* sport columnist and widely read "sage of the prairie," reported in 1952 having seen the brothers on separate occasions at Chicago Stadium.

"When I was in Chicago to see Sugar Ray Robinson fight," Coughlin began his item, "Bob Goodman was in the press row. He said he was covering the fight for the *Police Gazette*. When I seen (Chuck) Davey fight down there Irwin Goodman was in the press row. I asked him who he was covering the fight for he said the *Ladies Home Journal*."

Roundy's prose rarely bothered with punctuation or syntax, and of course he knew Bob and Irwin weren't really covering the fights for anyone. They were in press row because they knew a lot of press people with credentials. In Chicago, it may even have been Roundy who provided them.

Seiko and Elgin made fine watches and the Goodmans had good relationships with both manufacturers, but for years, according to wholesaler Arlon Mason, Bob and Irwin very much wanted to sell Rolex watches in their State Street store.

"Wearing a Rolex is making a statement," Mason said. It was, and probably still is, the gold standard for wrist watches. But Rolex does not let just anyone market their merchandise.

There can be no greater testimony to Belle's enduring influence on Bob and Irwin than in the wide ranging philanthropy that became such a major part of their lives.

One day in the 1980s, Bob Goodman called Mason. "How can we get Rolex?" Bob said.

Mason told the Goodmans that the secret to getting Rolex was to attend the large jewelry and watch trade show held annually in Basel, Switzerland. Today the Basel show brings 1,800 companies and over 100,000 visitors from the trade together. It was the biggest show in the world in the 1980s, when Mason suggested the Goodmans attend.

Mason knew a bit about the haughty way Rolex conducted business. He made an unusual suggestion to Bob Goodman.

"I told Bob, 'Fly to Basel for the show, and take with you a cashier's check made out to Rolex for a quarter of a million dollars. You do that because they are going to look at you and tell you their minimum opening order is $250,000. And they will tell you that you can't pick the styles.'"

Mason said he advised Bob to listen to the story, and then pull the check for $250,000 from his pocket and say, "OK, ship the product."

It sounds like the kind of great story that may well have been varnished and improved over the years, but Mason insists it's true.

"That's just what happened," Mason said. "Bob handed them the check. He said, 'We'll trust you with the styles. Ship them out.' And they got the product in, and knocked everybody dead with it."

A real death—the unexpected passing of their mother, Belle Abrahamson Goodman—rocked Bob and Irwin in the summer of 1961. The front page headline of *The Capital Times*, August 26, 1961, read: "Mrs. Harry Goodman, 66, Madison Civic Leader, Dies."

The secondary headline read: "Mother of Jewelers."

The story, accompanied by a photo of Belle Abrahamson Goodman in a stylish black hat, mentioned how she had moved to Madison with her husband in 1940, and it stressed her charitable work.

"She had spent hundreds of hours as a Gray Lady, Green Lady, and Red Cross aide serving in Madison hospitals and as a volunteer worker at the Dane County Home, Verona," the story noted. "During World War II she was a 'mother away from home' to many service men stationed here."

The story listed her many affiliations, including the Woman's Club, United Givers Association, Council of Jewish Women, Eastern Star, Temple Beth El Sisterhood, and the Madison Jewish Welfare Council." Along with her sons, she was survived by a sister and four brothers.

Just as he had at the funeral of Harry Goodman, Rabbi Manfred Swarsensky of Temple Beth El officiated at Belle's funeral. She was buried next to her husband in Madison's Forest Hill Cemetery.

There is no overstating the importance of Belle in the lives of her sons. She was a large personality who commanded respect, and expected achievement, grace and a commitment to the greater good from her sons. She got all that, starting with personal respect.

"The one thing that most characterizes Irwin to me is the way he treated our mother," Bob said a quarter century after Belle's death. "We'd go someplace and when we entered the elevator, Irwin would take off his hat. Most men, at that time, would take off their hats for other women, but Irwin is the only man I ever knew who treated his mother with that kind of respect."

There can be no greater testimony to Belle's enduring influence on Bob and Irwin than in the wide ranging philanthropy that became such a major part of their lives after their mother's death.

Yet it seems fair, too, to wonder if such a dominant personality didn't also play a role in personal decisions the sons made during her lifetime, decisions regarding women, marriage, and children.

"Their mother was so important to them," said a close friend of the Goodmans, noting that as he understood it, each brother was engaged to be married at least once. One theory as to why the engagements didn't result in marriage was that Belle did not approve.

One family member said, "There are family stories that nobody has been able to verify. There were stories that they were engaged. There was a story that one of them had been married for a short time, and that marriage was annulled. The real truth is probably only something they and their mother knew, and no one else."

Others would point out that the fact neither married allowed Bob and Irwin to form a close and loving relationship that may have been unique among brothers.

Bob's and Irwin's cousin Susan Hill would sometimes wonder if they regretted not marrying and having children—they were so good with hers, so interested in how the Hill kids were doing—but Susan could also see the flip side of that coin.

"They may have realized that had they gone that route they wouldn't have grown so close to each other—and they really, truly watched out for each other—or necessarily led the kind of lives they had been able to lead. I don't think they had regrets, really."

Bob and Irwin did enjoy young people. "They loved our kids," Hill said. "They liked watching them grow up. If they didn't attend one of their functions, they'd call and ask how things went."

When Susan's daughter got married, the couple asked that in lieu of gifts, donations be made to a hunger project. "Irwin phoned," Hill recalled. "In fact, I think that was the last time I spoke with Irwin. He wanted to know more about what the hunger project was. He thought it was wonderful they weren't asking for gifts. And that was the last time I talked to him. He sounded

good and strong and I told him so. He said if he kept talking, that wouldn't be the case. He said he couldn't talk very long without getting tired."

Longtime friend Ghita Bessman recalled how much Bob and Irwin loved to hear her granddaughter, Ariel, an accomplished pianist, play the piano. Even when they were no longer getting out, the brothers would call on Sunday mornings, and listen over the telephone while Ariel played.

One morning Irwin called an hour earlier than usual. He seemed especially anxious to hear Ariel play, which, of course, she did. It was later that day, Ghita recalled, when Irwin died.

Jewish Social Services of Madison

CONNECTIONS

Newsletter Sponsored by the Anna & Oscar Bentley Fund   Summer 2003, Vol. 3, No. 1

Belle Goodman
A Brilliant Jewel in Madison's Crown
BY BARBARA SPERER, JSS Associate Executive Director

Faces of philanthropy: Belle passed down a legacy of service to her sons Robert and Irwin Goodman.

Like so many organizations and institutions in the Madison community, Jewish Social Services is blessed to count on Irwin and Robert Goodman as generous benefactors. Over the last twenty-five years, the Goodmans have always been there for us.

They provided the seed money for the Financial Assistance Program, which provides grants for people with short-term, emergency needs. Because of them, a runaway teenager has gotten a bus ticket back to her parents, a senior has been able to purchase medicine he couldn't afford, a young family facing eviction has been given time to remain in their home, an out-of-work person has avoided having their heat cut off. And that is just the beginning.

The Goodmans remember JSS every year during the Friends campaign, they offer help spontaneously and they've taken significant steps to ensure our future – and the well-being of those who need help years from now – by establishing an endowment fund.

Try to thank the Goodmans for their philanthropy and they will tell you that it is their mother, Belle Goodman, who deserves the credit; it was her compelling example that led them to share the fruits of their success with the community they love, and that is why they chose to endow the Temple Beth El religious school wing in her memory.

Belle Goodman was born October 26, 1894, in St. Paul, Minnesota. She died in Madison on August 25, 1961. Unfortunately, none of her contemporaries are still with us, but their children are, and we sought out their recollections of this impressive woman. Her *yahrzeit* (anniversary of her death) seems a fitting time for a remembrance.

Goodman Jewelers opened in 1933 and the Goodmans lived at Quisling Towers at One East Gilman Street off the Capitol Square.

Joe Silverberg, whose mother Rose was a good friend, told us that the "tall, stately woman" came to Madison in the 1930s to be near her sons.

Anita Parks, another lifelong Madisonian, remarked, "Everyone thought she was the most gorgeous, elegant lady in the world." Anita went on to say that "Belle was a role model, not only for her sons, but for all the women in the community. She set the example and is responsible for what her sons are today." Adding a touch of the times, she noted, "Mrs. Goodman made the world's greatest apple pie out of Ritz crackers!"

Ida Swarsensky, wife of the late Rabbi Manfred Swarsensky (founding rabbi of Temple Beth El), commented that she "never heard a negative word about Belle Goodman." Ida called her "a real lady" and admired Mrs. Goodman's devotion to volunteer work — particularly her visits to the local boarding school for handicapped children and how Belle remembered the youngsters' birthdays and other important occasions. Belle was, "sweeter than sugar, a lady to the nth degree."

Temple Beth El secretary Shirley Sweet was a young married woman when she met Belle Goodman. Shirley remembers her fondly as "very philanthropic, a woman who joined every service organization."

And so, we say "thank you" to Belle Goodman. Thanks for the charitable acts, the *mitzvot* that you performed in your own right. But, thanks also for raising two *menschen*, two quality human beings, with such an unabiding sense of *tzedakah*, righteousness, that they have provided the Jewish community and Dane County with two lifetimes filled with countless acts of immeasurable generosity.

inside

Elder Abuse 2

Farewell and Welcome 10

Tribute Donors and Friends of JSS 3, 9

Russian Corner 11

Volunteer Connection 12

The summer 2003 issue of the newsletter for Jewish Social Services of Madison paid tribute to Belle Goodman, the most significant influence on the lives of Bob and Irwin Goodman.

CHAPTER 4
Rotarians and Sportsmen

In the early 1960s, not long after their mother's death, Bob and Irwin made an association that would loom large in their lives for nearly half a century.

The Rotary Club of Madison, commonly referred to as Downtown Rotary, was established in 1913. The population of Madison was not yet 30,000, and the club's first meeting brought together eight men in an electrical supply store on King Street.

The club would eventually grow to 500 members, placing Downtown Rotary among the top ten largest Rotary clubs in the world. Women were first allowed in Rotary Clubs worldwide in 1987, and Downtown Rotary quickly encouraged women to join. As Downtown Rotary approached its centennial anniversary in 2013, the club could claim that seven of the past twenty-one club presidents had been women. In 1997, Dr. Perry Henderson became the first black president of Downtown Rotary.

Bob and Irwin applauded that diversity. Such inclusiveness was in keeping with the club's philanthropic goals, something Downtown Rotary took seriously enough for the Goodmans to use Rotary as a vehicle for a portion of their personal philanthropy, through generous gifts to the Downtown Rotary Foundation.

For the Goodmans, the association with Rotary began in May of 1962, when Madison attorney Dick Stroud wrote a letter to the Rotary Club of Madison.

"Enclosed is an application form completed for Irwin A. Goodman, together with his check for $35.00, a picture, and a completed questionnaire."

Among the notable points on the questionnaire, Irwin listed his nickname as "Irv" and his hobbies as "tennis, swimming, paddle ball and travel."

Naturally, if Irwin joined Rotary—and he was, of course, accepted—Bob was not going to be far behind. Less than three months later, on Sept. 5, 1962, Bob's application for membership arrived at the Rotary Club of Madison's offices at 122 West Washington Avenue.

Bob listed his hobbies as "tennis, paddle ball, softball, travel and reading."

For nearly the next 50 years, Rotary played a significant role in the lives of Bob and Irwin. They enjoyed the camaraderie of the weekly club luncheons, held in later years at the Inn on the Park, a short walk from their apartment. The Rotary files include letters of explanation from the brothers when travel or poor health required they miss a meeting. Also on file is a 1991 letter to the club from a vice president of First Wisconsin Bank, alert-

Bob and Irwin were avid Rotarians, joining Madison Downtown Rotary in 1962.

ing Downtown Rotary that Bob and Irwin were gifting the club 900 shares of Liz Claiborne Inc. stock worth nearly $45,000 and 250 shares of Merck & Co. stock worth more than $27,000. The stock was transferred to the Madison Rotary Foundation.

Perhaps the last piece of correspondence between Bob and Irwin and Rotary, and certainly the most poignant, came in January 2009, near the end, after the club had sent flowers to the brothers along with a holiday greeting.

"We are doing very well given our ages," Bob and Irwin wrote, after expressing thanks for the flowers and good wishes. They noted that they were following events in Madison and keeping up with sports, with special interest in all Badger athletic teams. "We don't get out much anymore and we don't have the stamina to attend meetings, but we can tell you that on every Wednesday (the day of the weekly lunch meetings) we think of all of you and wish it was possible to be among special friends

again. Thank you for your thoughtfulness, the flowers and specially hearing from you brightened our day." The letter was hand signed by Bob and Irwin.

"They loved Rotary," said Gordon Derzon, whose career included a lengthy term as president and CEO of the University of Wisconsin Hospital and Clinics. The Goodmans sponsored Derzon as a member of Downtown Rotary.

"They enjoyed the fellowship," Derzon said. "They thought it was a wonderful organization."

An indication of the brothers' affection for Rotary and the Wednesday lunches had come some years earlier when Downtown Rotary decided to publish a book of the wit and wisdom of its members. In the 1990s Rotary began asking members to write a check to the Rotary Foundation on their birthday—at least as many dollars as years old. At the meeting when the check was presented, the birthday celebrant was also allowed to provide a couple of lines—inspirational, humorous, member's choice—which would be read aloud by the club president.

In 2001, Downtown Rotary decided to collect those short messages into a book titled, *The Birthday Book, or Rotarians Say the Darnedest Things*.

Among the quotes was this from Mary Lang Sollinger, active in any number of good causes in the city: "I try to be the person my dog thinks I am."

UW law professor Gordon Baldwin also opted for humor: "Give a man a fish and he will eat for a day. Teach him how to fish and he will sit in a boat and drink beer all day."

Bob and Irwin's contribution to the Rotary birthday book was to pick up the entire cost of its printing and publication.

It was a not untypical gesture. While the major "naming" gifts that occurred later in the brothers' lives will always be their main legacy—what the city collectively will remember them for—the brothers for decades made smaller gifts, sometimes completely anonymously, often with little attendant publicity, that made a great difference in the lives of the recipients.

One that did get a bit of press came in the summer of 1972, when a UW track athlete, Big 10 Conference triple jump champion Patrick Onyango of Kenya, found himself unable to travel to the Summer Olympics in Munich because of a lack of funds. It had been assumed that Onyango would not compete because no Kenyan athletes were going to compete after the International Olympic Committee invited segregated Rhodesia to participate. At the last minute, Rhodesia's invitation was withdrawn. Many African nations, including Kenya, found themselves scrambling not only to field teams but to finance the travel of their athletes. Onyango received word in Madison that he could participate if he could get to Germany on his own.

Originally UW athletic director Elroy Hirsch had thought his department could provide the travel expenses, but a Big 10 rule prohibited it. Regulations also prevented the Winged Foot Club—the UW track team's booster group—from helping.

UW athletic department officials quietly approached the Goodmans. The brothers' passion for the Olympics was well known. In April, Bob and Irwin, along with

Bob with Del Crandall, a Brewers manager during the 1970s. Bob and Irwin enjoyed attending games in Milwaukee.

Madison banking executive Collie Ferris, had served as co-chairmen for a Dane County luncheon that raised funds for the U.S. Olympic Committee. It was held at the Park Motor Inn (the same hotel that hosted Rotary and became the Inn on the Park) and it drew no less celebrated an athlete than Jesse Owens, who gave the keynote speech. Owens was the perfect speaker in advance of the 1972 Munich Games—36 years earlier, in another Olympics in Munich, Owens had won four gold medals. Not surprisingly, when the Kenyan situation presented itself a few months later, the Goodmans stepped up, and Onyan-

Bob and Irwin with Bob Rennebohm, who served as president of the University of Wisconsin Foundation.

a meaningful involvement in athletics is a tremendous source of happiness and fulfillment. The privilege of working in behalf of our great University of Wisconsin, with dedicated people like Elroy (Hirsch) and Otto (Breitenbach) and so many here, is richly rewarding. And now, receiving the Pat O'Dea Award here tonight, with all it stands for, makes us very happy and very proud. Bob and I want you to know we are deeply honored."

A few months later, a note arrived at the jewelry store, addressed to Bob and Irwin. "Dear Irv and Bob, It seems as though I am always writing to you, thanking you for something or other. If it's not for a personal favor, it's for your outstanding generosity."

Athletic Director Elroy "Crazylegs" Hirsch was writing to thank them for picking up the cost of the track team's year end banquet. "As I have said many times before," Hirsch wrote, "I only wish we had more like you. "Once again, my deepest thanks." Hirsch hand-signed it with his nickname: "Legs."

Another letter from around the same time that Bob and Irwin saved in their files came from a sports name that would eventually nearly equal Elroy Hirsch. Later, Bud Selig would spend many years as the commissioner of Major League Baseball. When he wrote Bob and Irwin in January, 1973, he was president of the fledgling new team in Milwaukee named the Brewers. The Goodmans had watched in dismay with the rest of the state when the Braves decamped for Atlanta several years earlier. Now the Brewers had taken their place and were trying to sell themselves to the state of Wisconsin. UW baseball coach Dynie Mansfield had invited the Goodmans to be early members of the Brewers' Madison booster club and Selig was writing in hopes they'd attend a meeting in Madison.

"I'm delighted to have the opportunity to tell the story of the Brewers to the business leaders of the Madison area," Selig wrote. "Even though your schedule must be very crowded, I do hope you will be able to attend and that I'll have the chance to meet you."

Bob and Irwin became devoted fans of the Brewers. Over the years they would invite friends to games—the friends often providing transportation—in Milwaukee.

Gordon Derzon recalled how he and his wife, Gail,

go competed in the Munich games. In an interview, Bob said he hoped it might encourage the Kenyan government to allow more of its athletes to come to Wisconsin.

"We feel that in making it possible for this fine young athlete to compete for his country in the Olympics," Bob said, "we are hopefully insuring warmer relations between the University of Wisconsin and the Kenyan government, without whose approval and assistance no athlete can come to Wisconsin."

Less than two years later in June 1974, the Goodmans' contribution to UW athletics was formally recognized when the brothers received the Pat O'Dea Award, named for a transcendent Badger football player of the early 20th century. The award, presented annually by the Madison Pen and Mike Club and the Bowman Sports Foundation, went to individuals making a "significant contribution" to the UW athletic program.

Irwin and Bob accepted the award at a banquet at Madison's Holiday Inn. Irwin addressed the crowd: "All of us have our own definitions of what constitutes happiness and fulfillment. Speaking for Bob and myself,

THE UNIVERSITY OF WISCONSIN
DIVISION OF INTERCOLLEGIATE ATHLETICS

ELROY HIRSCH
Director of Athletics

February 1, 1985

Messrs. Irv and Bob Goodman
220 State Street
Madison, Wi 53703

Dear Irv and Bob:

I'm sorry I am so late in getting this note off to you but, as you know, we left for the Hall of Fame Bowl on December 25th and then Ruth and I visited our son on the west coast following the game and then went on for a vacation on the Island of Maui. We left Maui when it was 84°, stepped off the plane here some sixteen hours later to 27° below -- a 111° drop, which is something my poor, old, frail body cannot stand. However, I am now recovering and am now getting around to the unanswered mail which has accumulated on my desk.

You two gentlemen have been so wonderful to me over the past sixteen years that words just can't describe it. I do want you to know, however, how much I deeply appreciate your friendship and all your wonderful support for the Department.

Needless to say, if there is anything I can ever do for you, you need but pick up the phone and ask.

Ruth will be wearing the gold heart pin proudly and I will wear my gold tie pin equally so and always with the knowledge that I know it came from two very, very good friends. Once again, my deepest thanks.

Sincerely,

Elroy L. Hirsch
Director of Athletics

ELH:pj

1440 MONROE STREET ● MADISON, WISCONSIN 53706 ● 608/262-1866
THE BADGERS ARE ON THE MOVE!

The Goodmans' generosity to UW athletics was greatly appreciated, as indicated by this letter from Elroy Hirsch.

Bob and Irwin at the site of the plaque marking the jogging path they helped create, one of their many philanthropic endeavors.

enjoyed driving Bob and Irwin to Milwaukee for the games. Gordon would drive and Gail would sit in the back seat with one of the brothers, while the other brother sat up front with Gordon. On the way back, the brothers would switch places.

"And whoever was sitting next to Gail," Gordon recalled, "would spend much of the drive telling her how wonderful their brother was. They were so close, just crazy about each other. Irv, God bless him, would always laugh at Bob's corny jokes."

Derzon and others would recall that each time they passed a cemetery going to the Brewers' games, Bob would say, "People are dying to get in there." And Irwin—always—would laugh.

John Hayes, the longtime employee who eventually bought the jewelry store from the Goodmans, also remembered attending Brewers games with the brothers and recalled that no matter how poorly the team played—and they had some lean years—Bob and Irwin would find a silver lining.

One game, the Brewers were losing by a wide margin in the eighth inning, and Irwin leaned over to Bob said, "You want to leave early?" Bob said, "Yeah."

Hayes recalled that as they began the drive home, Bob said, "Well, at least we didn't see them lose."

Hayes laughed. "It was typical of how they always had a good positive outlook about stuff. You never really saw them get down about anything. They were upbeat."

Bud Selig in his letter had identified the Goodmans as business leaders, and by the 1970s, Bob and Irwin Goodman were, by any measure, pillars not only of the Madison business community, but the city at large. Each was given an informal validation in the early years of the decade when they were featured, separately, in the *Wisconsin State Journal's* "Know Your Madisonian" column. To be included was to be recognized as a mover and shaker in Madison.

Irwin was first, profiled in December 1971.

"A handsome bachelor," the piece began, "who spends his business hours surrounded by diamonds and rubies, Irwin Goodman could, if he wished, lead the existence of royalty." Instead, the paper noted, Irwin "spends his time promoting the civic concerns of Madison and the surrounding area."

This profile of Irwin may have been the first time the general public was truly made aware of the extent of the Goodmans' devotion to both civic and charitable causes.

The piece noted of Irwin: "He is a director of Methodist Hospital and the Methodist Hospital Foundation, a past member of the Mayor's Commission on Human Rights, a member of the civic auditorium committee for the city and a director of the YMCA Foundation."

The piece continued: "One would think those activities would keep Goodman too busy to run his store. But in addition to them he is a director of the Madison Jewish Welfare Council, Temple Beth El, a member of the University of Wisconsin Foundation and the university's President's Club, and is active in the Zor Shrine, Masonic Lodge No. 5, the Downtown Rotary Club, and the National Olympics Committee."

When Irwin did speak about the jewelry business, his comments reflected both how long he had been in business and the value of the customer service he prized so highly.

"One of the biggest thrills in this business," Irwin said, "is seeing a young man come in and buy an engagement ring for his fiancée, dealing with him over the years, and then one day seeing his son come in to buy a ring for his own fiancée."

Two years later—January 1974—Bob was the subject of the "Know Your Madisonian" feature in the *State Journal*.

Much like the piece on Irwin, Bob's civic commitment was featured prominently, and he opened up on his love for the city that had now been home for more than 35 years.

"I love Madison," Bob said, "and I very much like the people in Madison. I do everything I can to help our city. I am dedicated to the fact that the central city and the downtown are strong and will be strong. State Street has a charm to us. We love the street."

Over the years Bob and Irwin received a number of awards from Downtown Rotary for their extraordinary service and generosity to Madison and the surrounding area.

In 1989, Rotary bestowed on the Goodmans its seventh annual Manfred E. Swarsensky Humanitarian Service Award, recognizing individuals who through their voluntary service have made outstanding civic contributions in the spirit of the late Rabbi Swarsensky.

The award was presented at the Nov. 8, 1989 Downtown Rotary lunch, and Bob and Irwin immediately donated the $1,000 honorarium to the United Way of Dane County.

In 1994, the Goodmans received Rotary's Senior Service Award. At the June luncheon where it was presented, club member Arlie Mucks—retired after many years as executive director of the Wisconsin Alumni Association—feigned astonishment that Bob and Irwin had yet to receive it.

"Senior Service Awards are for people who have given large amounts of civic or social service," Mucks said. "On that basis, we could give it to Bob and Irv every year."

Six years later, in August, 2000, Downtown Rotary—again at a Wednesday Inn on the Park lunch meeting—awarded Bob and Irwin the club's most prestigious

honor, the Werner Meritorious Service Award, named for the late Joseph G. Werner, a member of the Madison Rotary who was active in the club worldwide as an international director. The Werner Award is not an annual award but rather is given only when a member's service is truly distinguished.

"They've done so much for our club," Patricia Jenkins, executive director of Downtown Rotary, told the *Wisconsin State Journal*, "and really our community. This is our highest honor and so fitting."

Among the many Rotary-based projects funded by the Goodmans and cited at the luncheon were the 3.25 mile Rotary jogging path downtown and the Goodman-Rotary Senior Fitness Program, operated through the Madison School-Community Recreation Department. In 1994, the Goodmans seeded the program with a $200,000 endowment that eventually grew to $1 million and allowed MSCR to offer numerous exercise and nutrition classes, swimming, golf, tennis, ski and martial art instruction, as well as educational lectures.

The Goodmans would insist that nothing about their Rotary philanthropy made them special, as such civic engagement is a big part of Rotary's reason for being. But there was one aspect of the Wednesday lunches that was unique to Bob and Irwin. Beginning in the late 1960s, they made sure—just as they did at the other public venues they visited regularly for meals, such as the UW's Memorial Union—that a vegetarian option was always available.

The first most people in Madison knew about the Goodmans having embraced a healthy lifestyle likely came in a 1973 feature story in the *Wisconsin State Journal* that was headlined simply, "Dial-a-Dietician."

The story was written by John Newhouse, a celebrated Madison newspaperman who wrote a short biography of the Goodmans' colorful sports columnist friend, Joseph "Roundy" Coughlin. Newhouse's son, Eric, would also go into newspapers, and eventually won a Pulitzer Prize for a series of articles on alcoholism in Montana.

John Newhouse's feature story described a service that was a combined effort of the Madison Dietetic Association and Madison's Methodist Hospital. The service, Newhouse wrote, was called Dial-a-Dietician, and it was

Among the few luxuries Bob and Irwin afforded themselves was travel, often on cruise ships.

about weight control, but we don't know what to eat, or not to eat. Most of us don't really have vigorous good health, and diet, I'm sure, is an important part of feeling good all the time."

One day, after talking to Irwin, Marshall approached Joline Saunders, Methodist's head dietician, and mentioned the idea of some kind of telephone help line. Saunders immediately said it was something that had been discussed.

"It was a service we wanted to provide," she said, "but we lacked the money."

At which point Irwin and Bob Goodman said they would underwrite the cost of the program for three years.

When people called Dial-a-Dietician, someone would take down their question—they ran the gamut from nutritional content to healthy ways of preparing food—along with the caller's name and phone number. Within 24 hours, a member of the Madison Dietetic Association would call back with the answer to the question.

The program was a big hit. "We've seen how much diet has improved the health of people around us," Irwin said. He told the *State Journal* that over the last few years he had lost 40 pounds and that Bob lost 35. "We both feel a lot better for it," Irwin said.

In the last 40 years of their lives, promoting good health (and practicing what they preached) became a central component of the Goodmans' lifestyle. It was particularly true of Irwin. He lived it and he encouraged his friends to discover the benefits of eating well and exercising. It was important enough to Irwin that in a eulogy performed following Irwin's death, at 94, Rabbi Jonathan Biatch said the following:

"Another of his legacies was his focus on physical fitness and dieting. So many of his projects focused on improving the body in addition to the mind, that one could not help but feel pulled to physical excellence and development.

"Every time that I would visit," Rabbi Biatch continued, "Irwin was always interested in and concerned about my physical health, especially because of my career in the rabbinate, and especially after my automobile accident and injury. He would always inquire: 'Are you taking

the brainchild of Irwin Goodman.

Irwin served on the Methodist board of directors, and he had made a point of suggesting, more than once, to Methodist executive James Marshall that the hospital should offer people help choosing the right things to eat.

"Most people want and need to know more in this area, and don't know where to turn," Irwin told the *State Journal*. He continued: "Most of us are concerned

care of yourself? Are you exercising? What are you doing? How much time do you spend on that machine?' I understand that he politely inquired after the physical health of many of his friends, colleagues and visitors.

"As we know, Irwin was a vegan, always advocating the benefits of a strictly vegetarian lifestyle and shunning all animal products. And as if to prove his point that one could get a vegan meal anywhere he would have many a meal at Ponderosa Steak House, seeking an array of vegetarian selections from their salad bar. He was also very proud to demonstrate his industrial strength juicer, through which he could enjoy the fullness of his dietary choices.

"Overall," the rabbi concluded of Irwin, "his personal lifestyle represented a modesty and humility that should be an example to us who live in the society of consumption we have created."

For the record, Bob and Irwin liked the Ponderosa—on Madison's west side, across from the West Towne Mall, where they would also order a baked potato along with the salad bar—so much that the restaurant installed a plaque in their honor at their favorite booth.

As for the "juicer" referenced by Rabbi Biatch, the Goodmans' friend Gordon Derzon recalled: "They were constantly after us to buy one of these $350 blenders. Their big treat was to take these frozen bananas and put them through the blender. Actually they were pretty tasty." Other times, Derzon said, Bob and Irwin would ship him crates of mangoes and strawberries.

While Irwin was without doubt the point man for the brothers on health, Bob was on board, too. He gave an interview to the *Vegetarian Times* magazine in 1992 for an article on cruises.

"In 1970," Bob said, "when my brother and I started taking cruise vacations, vegan meant weird. Passengers would point to us as if we had a communicable disease. These days, tablemates see our whole-wheat pizza smothered with fresh tomato and basil, and right away they want it."

The magazine took note of the Goodmans' standard cruise fare: "The brothers start their cruise mornings with a bowl of tropical fruit along with their favorite buckwheat cereal, or nonfat yogurt and rye muffins. For dinner, they choose yams or baked potatoes instead of French fries, and they smother their vegetables with mashed avocado instead of butter."

In several interviews, Irwin dated the brothers' interest in a healthy lifestyle to 1967. That jives with several clippings in their files from *The Capital Times* newspaper from February 1967. One was headlined: "Stop Overeating—Start Living." It was part of a five-part series by a past president of the American Heart Association on the five steps to reduce a heart attack. The Goodmans saved two more articles from the series headlined "Active Man Usually Lives a Longer Life" and "It's Worth Watching Diet."

The same year Bob and Irwin clipped those newspaper stories they discovered, and embraced, a set of principles commonly referred to as Natural Hygiene.

The Goodmans saved in their files the January 1968

In the last 40 years of their lives, promoting good health (and practicing what they preached) became a central component of the Goodmans' lifestyle.

issue of a magazine called *Dr. Shelton's Hygienic Review*. In its pages, Dr. Herbert M. Shelton argued against medicinal cures and for a healthy lifestyle based on diet, exercise and austerity. The magazine included a full page advertisement for his new book, *Natural Hygiene: Man's Pristine Way of Life*.

It appears that the introduction of Bob and Irwin to the idea of Natural Hygiene came indirectly from Dr. Shelton himself. A Pennsylvania man named Joseph Reed, who began corresponding with Shelton when Reed was only 15 years old, was the man Bob and Irwin credited with getting them involved with Natural Hygiene. When Reed died in 1999, the magazine *Health Science*, a publication of the American Natural Hygiene Society (ANHS), published an obituary of Reed in which Reed said he had influenced many people to take up Natural Hygiene.

The magazine noted further: "At least two ANHS

Life members concur with that statement. Bob and Irwin Goodman of Madison, Wis. credit Joe with introducing them to Natural Hygiene and the American Natural Hygiene Society. The Goodmans recently gave a very generous gift to the Society in Joe's memory."

The year of Reed's introducing Natural Hygiene to the Goodmans was 1967. In 1998, Irwin gave an interview to *Health Science* magazine and said the following: "We first heard about Natural Hygiene in 1967. Since then, Natural Hygiene has become our way of life. Learning about Natural Hygiene has helped us to provide the kind of leadership in our community that we feel can benefit everyone."

The American Natural Hygiene Society was founded in 1948. In the late 1990s, the board of directors approved a name change to the National Health Association.

Although the organization formally dates only to the 1940s, Mark Huberman, a past president of the group, and a friend of Bob and Irwin Goodman, said that its principles go back at least a century prior to that.

"The movement goes back to the mid-1800s," Huberman said, "when a number of people were looking at the idea that health care is self-care, and the more natural foods you ate, the better you would be. They were ahead of their time."

The ideals of healthful living, Huberman said, really haven't changed a great deal since: vegetarian diet, fresh air, clean water, exercise, keeping your emotions in check.

Huberman is the chief magistrate of the domestic relations court of Mahoning County, Ohio. Huberman's interest in Natural Hygiene was handed down from his father, Max Huberman. Max credited Natural Hygiene with helping him beat polio when the disease struck when he was 30 years old. He accepted the tenets and called himself a Hygienist. It was 1958. He joined the ANHS, he and his wife started a mom and pop health food store that sold organic food and exercise equipment, and he started writing articles about food, health and consumer issues. And he taught the ways of Natural Hygiene to his son,

Mark, who embraced them.

In an interview, Mark Huberman said the Hygienist lifestyle is not the vegan lifestyle. "Vegan tends to have a kindness to animals bent to it," Huberman said. "Natural Hygience is more about the health of it. Those other things are bonuses. It is better for the environment, there is less cruelty to animals, but the fact is just because you don't eat meat doesn't make you healthy. You could still have all the processed food you wanted, all the salt and sugar."

According to Huberman, the Goodmans were well liked and respected within the Natural Hygiene movement. "They were public people but they really didn't proselytize" about Natural Hygiene, Huberman said. "If you asked, they would tell you."

Asked whether it was fair to categorize the Natural Hygience lifestyle as extreme, Huberman said, "I think what I would say, and the Goodmans would say, is that what others do is extreme. This is really pretty simple and pretty satisfying. It's satisfying not just to your palate but to your head."

He wished more had been made of the importance of the lifestyle in the stories written after Bob and Irwin died. "There was almost no mention of their healthy lifestyle in their obituaries and I think that missed the mark a little bit," Huberman said. "It really did define their existence. They traveled, but when they traveled they spent a good part of the time for many years at a clinic in Australia run by Dr. (Alec) Burton. They spent a lot of time at the Regency House Health Spa in Hallendale, Florida."

The Goodmans' files included stationery from the Regency House outlining their exercise regime when they stayed at the spa and also included a receipt from a three week stay in February and March 1998: the total bill, $7,987.24.

Natural Hygiene would remain a recipient of the Goodmans' largesse until their deaths. Mark Huberman concluded, "They both loved life. They shared their generosity with us, and they encouraged others to give."

CHAPTER 5
A Softball Diamond, and a Jewish Community Campus

The contention that natural hygiene and a healthy lifestyle "defined" Bob and Irwin Goodman, as Mark Huberman suggested, would have been more accurate had he said it was part of what defined them. The brothers were also defined by their love of family and each other; by their passion for athletics, particularly UW athletics; by their commitment to their State Street jewelry business; by their philanthropy, and a desire to give back to their adopted home city and people less fortunate than themselves; and also, significantly, they were defined by their commitment to the Jewish community in Madison and around the world.

"I think it was probably the most central part of their lives," said Steve Morrison, who spent, prior to his retirement in 2010, more than a quarter century as executive director of the Madison Jewish Community Council (MJCC), which in 2009 changed its name to the Jewish Federation of Madison.

Morrison, a native of Elgin, Illinois, came to Madison in 1984 from Washington, D.C. to run both the MJCC and Jewish Social Services.

"Because this is a small Jewish community," Morrison said, "they had one person directing both."

The Madison Jewish community may be relatively small, but it is vibrant. Jews first came to the city in the early 1850s, and in 1856 17 Jewish families formed Madison's first synagogue, known as Gates of Heaven, which is today a historic landmark in James Madison Park.

The Jewish population grew with the city and by the year 2000 there were an estimated 6,500 Jews living in the greater Madison area, along with nearly as many Jewish students attending the University of Wisconsin–Madison.

Morrison met the Goodmans shortly after he arrived in Madison in 1984.

"Someone in my position," Morrison said, "what you did is—within the first few weeks—go out and try to meet key leaders and contributors. Bob and Irwin were both."

The Goodmans greeted Morrison at their State Street jewelry store and invited him into their office at the back of the store.

"Right away I liked their warmth and informality,"

Morrison said. "At our first meeting, within a few minutes, they had asked me to go to a game, a Brewers game in Milwaukee. I told them I didn't like sports. 'How about a movie?' they said. I think they respected that I was honest about not liking sports."

From the outset, Morrison was impressed by the Goodmans' involvement in civic life.

"They knew everybody," he said. "If I mentioned someone I had met from the African-American community, they knew that person. Or I might mention I had

Bob and Irwin's involvement in the Madison Jewish communithy began early, and was influenced, like so much in their lives, by their mother, Belle.

been to a meeting about the Madison schools. Bob and Irwin would know the players, and I would hear long stories—which school superintendent really deserved the credit for this or that, and why."

It would then figure that the brothers were pleased when Morrison engaged the greater Madison community as well.

"They liked that I became involved in the community right away," Morrison said. "The people who held the job before me really never did. I've always felt the Jewish community needs to be involved in the general community. If we were involved with the NAACP or the Boys and Girls Club, some people might ask why we cared about that. Bob and Irwin liked that we did. They were my allies."

The Goodmans appreciated it when Morrison would write a guest column for the Madison papers on matters pertaining to Israel. In 1989, the plight of Jews in the Soviet Union was getting worldwide attention. Jews were persecuted in the Soviet Union, but neither were they allowed to leave. It was untenable. When the Soviet leader Mikhail Gorbachev visited Washington, D.C. that year, a massive demonstration was planned. Jews had never turned out in such numbers to protest. Madison sent a delegation of 70, most by bus, with protest signs and red

caps to help them stay together amid the throng, which eventually numbered 250,000. Quietly, with no publicity, Bob and Irwin paid for the bus, the caps and the signs. Morrison led the Madison contingent and when he got back, Irwin telephoned, wanting to hear about it. Gorbachev eventually lifted the travel restrictions on Jews.

Bob and Irwin's involvement in the Madison Jewish community began early, and was influenced, like so much in their lives, by their mother, Belle.

"Everything revolved around her," Al Goldstein said. "That's how they got involved in Jewish life."

Goldstein—well known in Madison as "Mr. G," the longtime proprietor of Carmen's clothing store—first met Bob and Irwin when he came to Madison in 1946.

"My uncle was in business and knew the Goodmans," Goldstein said. "The Jewish people would get together. Bob and Irwin already had developed a reputation. Everybody loved them. Nobody could say a word about them that wasn't good."

Of Bob and Irwin's involvement in Madison Jewish life, Goldstein said, "They participated. They didn't want to be the kingpins. They observed it, they contributed to it, and they helped it grow. Madison had a nice population of Jewish people, but not many of them were in the financial position that Bob and Irwin were. There were a couple others, but they didn't participate. The boys never said no to a worthwhile cause."

Goldstein said over the years Bob and Irwin were active with two Madison synagogues, Temple Beth El and the Beth Israel Center.

"They were members of both," Goldstein said. "They provided funds for both, too. They weren't overly religious. They would go to services and such, but they weren't orthodox. They were like me. We weren't reform, but we wanted to be part of it."

Steve Morrison concurred: "I can't say they were in any way religiously observant. They didn't keep kosher. They could have, given they were vegan. But they weren't raised in that tradition. They weren't regular synagogue goers. They were very knowledgeable Jews. They had a good Jewish education. It was clear to me in our early meetings that they were committed Zionists, long before the state of Israel existed. Not only did they give a significant amount through their philanthropy, both prior to the creation of the state of Israel and after, but they traveled there. They had friends and one Israeli cousin they were very close to. They were active in Jewish organizations early in their lives, as leaders and volunteers. As their mother had been."

The Madison Jewish Welfare Fund, the first incarnation of what is now the Jewish Federation of Madison, was formed in May, 1940. By 1953, Irwin was a member of its executive committee. In September of that year he was one of three committee members who bestowed a "certificate of appreciation" on Julius Ginsburg of Chicago in a ceremony at Madison's Loraine Hotel, in recognition of Ginsburg's service to Jewish communities across America. Irwin would remain a board member through the next several decades, even as the organization's name changed, first to the Madison Jewish Welfare Council and then the Madison Jewish Community Council.

In 1954, one of the organization's most enduring traditions—and one that would eventually benefit greatly from Bob and Irwin Goodman—began when 27 children participated in a summer program at two Madison parks, Vilas and Wingra. Two summers later, it would move to Olin Park, where it would remain for decades. The program was called Camp Shalom.

As Joel Minkoff remembers it, Camp Shalom may have started, at least in part, because he and his siblings needed something to do in the summer.

Minkoff is a third-generation executive at General Beverage and Beer, a venerable Madison firm founded in 1933. His grandfather Max Weinstein founded the company. Weinstein was likewise involved in the formation of the organization that is now the Madison Jewish Federation. He passed along his passion for both to his children and their families. Max's daughter, Evelyn, married a man named Ben Minkoff.

In 1984, on the 30th anniversary of the founding of Camp Shalom, the *Wisconsin State Journal* ran a story titled "Camp Shalom—30 years of touching lives."

The story noted the camp's origins: "In organizing the camp in 1954 the (Jewish Community Welfare) coun-

Bob and Irwin at a celebration of Camp Shalom's 40th Anniversary at Olin Park.

cil acted on a suggestion from member Ben Minkoff, who has continued his interest in the program."

Joel Minkoff was three years old at the time, but he was there, and he remembers.

"We were three boys and a girl in my parents' household," Minkoff said. "We were very, very active kids. My mother went so far as to say to my dad, 'If you don't find a place for these kids to go in the summer, then I am going to go work in the office, and you can stay home with these children.'"

Minkoff chuckled. "The next summer, Camp Shalom started."

It was successful from the start.

Joel Minkoff recalled: "What began as a small group started to grow and evolve. People would say, 'Is it just for Jewish kids?' My father felt very strongly it should be for all kids. It was a program that was started and developed by the Jewish community, but it was for everybody.

Camp Shalom in the 1990s
at Olin Park.

"Many of my childhood friendships developed through Camp Shalom," Minkoff continued. "That was the focus. Meeting families, having picnics, taking the buses back and forth each day, singing songs, packing lunches, swimming in Lake Monona. Swimming and learning to swim was a big part of camp. We cleaned and did chores, boys and girls sharing equally. It was multicultural and meant to bring people together."

Years passed, word of the camp's success got around, and more kids wanted to participate. It began to stretch the capacity of Olin Park, the site since 1956. By the 1970s, there were long waiting lists.

"My father hated waiting lists," Joel Minkoff said. "They had peaked camp out at about 50 kids. As I got involved, I asked why there were 10 or 15 kids on a waiting list. Why was there a waiting list at all? Well, there were some kids who couldn't pay. I said, 'Let's create scholarship money.' It went up to 75 kids. They said that's all they could handle."

Bob and Irwin Goodman had created an endowment

with (what would become) the Madison Jewish Federation that in part helped provide the scholarship money.

Organization director Steve Morrison was impressed by how the endowment—one of several provided by the Goodmans—operated.

"In those days," Morrison said, "endowment funds were kind of a new business. I was intrigued by the requirements they put in. Only 75 percent of the earnings could be used in any one year. And only earnings could be used. They were saying the fund should grow. It shouldn't be used up. They didn't say what it should be used for. They trusted the volunteers to make those decisions."

By the 30th anniversary in 1984, the camp had grown to two three-week sessions, with some 145 kids at each session. Twenty-six kids received scholarship assistance.

By 1994, and the 40th anniversary, the number of campers had grown to 600 across three, three-week sessions at Olin Park. There was a "regular" Camp Shalom and another for middle school kids who were allowed trips to the Wisconsin Dells and Milwaukee Brewers games, along with an expectation that they provide community service.

On the occasion of the 40th anniversary, some former campers told the *State Journal* what the experience had meant to them, including David Clarenbach, a well-known former state legislator in Madison.

"Beyond a doubt," Clarenbach said, "it left one of the greatest impressions of any youthful experience. It was a wonderful melting pot, with kids from all parts of town and all walks of life."

A man named Tom Kaufman, who was first a camper and later a counselor at Camp Shalom—not an unusual circumstance—said, "It was and still is a place where kids come first. The staff really makes an effort to integrate Jewish culture with ordinary camp life. They try very hard to hire staff with expertise in child care and teaching, and the quality of the staff is reflected in the quality of the camp program."

Steve Morrison recalled that beyond the endowment that assisted with scholarships for Camp Shalom, Bob and Irwin Goodman expressed interest in helping find a site, other than a city park, for the camp.

The Goodman Jewish Community Campus in Verona, which includes the current site of Camp Shalom.

"Very early on," Morrison said, "they started talking to me about Camp Shalom. They said, 'You're at Olin. Don't you need your own place?'"

Joel Minkoff, meanwhile, was on the council committee overseeing Camp Shalom, a committee he would eventually chair.

"There was some discussion about finding a new site," Minkoff said, dating the talks back to the 1980s. "At the executive committee meeting, I kept talking about starting a site fund. They asked how much money I thought we could raise. I said, 'Let's start and see.' We had been talking about the limitations of Olin Park, the need for growth, and a site fund so we could set money aside. There was a lot of discussion and they finally allowed us to start putting $10 per camper set aside for the fund." Eventually it would be $25 per camper, and the fund would grow close to six figures.

Joel Minkoff and Steve Morrison began touring Dane County, looking for potential sites.

"We went everywhere," Minkoff said, "looking at everything that was possible. Steve Morrison is not an outdoors type person. We would trudge through marshes and he would yell at me. But we had fun together, too. Rain, snow, mud. We had a very active group involved."

Morrison would recall the day in 1998, when he and Minkoff happened on what they felt was the site they had been seeking.

"We were driving around looking for farms that were for sale in Verona," Morrison said. "I took a wrong turn and we saw a for sale sign. We drove onto a dirt road and onto the property." One good omen: They knew the real estate agent. Her kids had attended Camp Shalom.

"Joel and I walked around a bit," Morrison said. "We saw this big open field. We thought we saw water." Within a day or two, the real estate agent gave Morrison and Minkoff a tour. The more they saw, the more they liked it. It would eventually include 154 acres.

"We looked at the place and got all excited," Minkoff recalled.

Of course, it would not come cheaply.

"We knew if we were talking about buying property we were talking about seven figures," Morrison said. "Up until then, no one was even giving six figures. There were people giving mid-five figures on an annual basis."

Joel Minkoff went to visit Lawrence Weinstein, who was ill, too ill to visit the property. Lawrence said, "You need to talk to the Goodmans. Show the Goodmans."

Steve Morrison had an excellent relationship with Bob and Irwin. Minkoff saw them less frequently, but they were friendly. Some years before, in his capacity as

Bob and Irwin at the ground-breaking for the women's softball diamond they helped make possible.

president of Hillel, the Jewish organization on the UW–Madison campus, Minkoff had approached the Goodmans about sponsoring a fund-raising run. It was a good fit. Bob and Irwin had supported Hillel over the years, and they were committed to physical fitness. Together they came up with the idea for the Goodman Runs. They were held for several years in the late 1980s and early '90s. The first year it was up and down State Street, and then they moved to the lake shore path.

"Everyone was shocked they let us use their name for the run," Minkoff said. He felt Bob and Irwin got a kick out of it, even allowing their photos to be used on the race T-shirts. The runs raised money for Hillel and were a success all around.

Now, a decade later, and a week after Morrison and Minkoff first saw the Verona farm property, the two men invited Bob and Irwin out to see it.

"By then," Morrison recalled, "they were resisting a lot of driving and walking around. It was especially hard on Irwin's legs. But they came."

"Steve set it up," Minkoff said. "We met out there."

It went well from the start. "I can't remember if it was Bob or Irwin," Minkoff said, "but we were in the house, looking out over the field, and I said, 'Could you imagine having 200 campers out there?' He looked at me and said, 'No, I could see at least 300 campers.'"

Minkoff eventually left to go back to work at General Beverage. Morrison, Bob and Irwin went to the Ponderosa Steak House for lunch.

"It was then, right then and there," Morrison said, "that they made a commitment to buy. They didn't even ask the price. They said they wanted to buy it for us."

Morrison voiced his deep appreciation, but added, "It's a lot of money."

One of the brothers said, "How much?"

Morrison said, "The asking price is $1.25 million."

According to Morrison, Bob and Irwin said, "How about if we give you a million and a half? That way you'll have some extra money."

It was an extraordinary gift. Minkoff remembers Morrison being so excited to tell him that he "almost ran me over in the parking lot."

The money was officially pledged and accepted at the Madison Jewish Community Council board of directors meeting on December 15, 1998.

At the meeting, the board expressed its gratitude to Bob and Irwin. There was a champagne toast. Someone asked about upkeep for the property—it's located at the northeast corner of County Route PD and Timber Lane—and Minkoff mentioned the small fee that had been assessed to every camper at Camp Shalom in recent years. That site fund stood at $90,000, and it could be targeted for upkeep. The gift was announced publicly the following August. Both Madison daily newspapers carried stories, including the news that the new facility would be called the Irwin A. and Robert D. Goodman Jewish Community Campus.

Madison attorney Willie Haus, president of the Madison Jewish Community Council, told the *Capital Times*, "This might be the best thing the Goodmans ever did, and they've done a lot of good things around here."

That Bob and Irwin allowed their names to be used was significant.

"It took me a long time to convince them to use their names," Morrison said. "I kept saying to them, 'Naming isn't a bad thing. Doing it anonymously is wonderful, but once you go out front and allow us to name it, it allows us to publicly thank you, and along with that, it becomes kind of a model for others.' So they went along with it, and people wanted to give to it to honor the Goodmans."

Joel Minkoff saw the value of the Goodman name during negotiations on zoning and other matters as work began to make the campus a reality.

"Everybody loved the Goodmans," Minkoff said. "Normally there would have been conservatives and liberals at each other's throats. When this project came forward, everybody was trying to find a way to honor the Goodmans, and make it happen. The neighbors were the same. The fact Bob and Irwin were involved helped allow it to happen."

Bob with head coach Karen Gallagher at opening day of the Goodman Diamond.

The campus was dedicated with a ceremony on August 22, 1999. The Jewish community had held an annual summer picnic at Elver Park and the decision was made to have it at the new property, along with the dedication. It was a Sunday and hundreds of people showed up. There were reporters and television cameras.

"It was very exciting," Morrison said. "Bob was beaming. He was very modest. He didn't want to speak."

The *State Journal* article the following day noted: "Plans call for an aquatic center, an indoor sports facility, sports fields, nature trails, gardens, theaters, education centers, sledding hills and a pond for fishing and ice skating."

As work on the campus moved forward, Bob and Irwin stayed involved.

"They watched pretty closely," Minkoff said. "They

wanted to know what was going on."

Morrison concurred. "As we were developing the master plan," he said, "I met more and more frequently with Irwin and Bob, usually in the office across the hall from their apartment. The desk was their mother's dining room table and it was piled with all the awards they'd been given and all the T-shirts and hats they'd been given by various organizations.

Even while the varsity baseball program still existed, the Goodmans had expressed an interest in the possiblity of UW adding softball as a women's sport.

"We reviewed plan after plan after plan," Morrison continued. "Bob and Irwin would ask that other people get involved—other donors besides just them—but whenever they made suggestions, it was very gentle. "

Irwin and Bob came to the official opening of the new campus. They posed for photos and couldn't help but bask in the glow of warm feelings. Later, as the campers came, Morrison and others would share their stories, sometimes on video with Bob and Irwin. Morrison recalled one in particular. A boy from the former Soviet Union came to Camp Shalom on just his second day in Madison. He was scared of thunder, and sure enough, a big storm blew through. The boy was petrified but there was someone on the Camp Shalom staff who spoke Russian and was able to calm him.

Everyone was welcome. Several Muslim kids enjoyed the camp. It was extraordinary. A *State Journal* article in 2003 called the campers "a diverse group that looks like the United Nations of Dane County and beyond."

The next summer would be Camp Shalom's 50th anniversary. The newspaper noted that along with the aquatic center the Goodman campus now had "a year round use multipurpose center, basketball courts, an improved entrance with parking, groomed trails for walking, bicycling or cross-country skiing, and ball fields" in development.

Like so much in Madison, it wouldn't have happened without Bob and Irwin Goodman.

"You can never say thank you enough," Joel Minkoff observed, one December day in 2012. "The acts of kindness and generosity that they have shown to this community, I'm not sure enough people really understand or respect it. I hope they do."

While some people recall the Goodman campus as the brothers' first significant naming gift, that honor actually goes to the softball diamond at the University of Wisconsin that Bob and Irwin helped make a reality a few years earlier.

That Bob and Irwin would make a large gift to UW athletics was not, of course, surprising. Their close association with the program has been noted throughout this book. They were valued enough to have been invited to travel on road trips with the football team. Among the papers saved by the Goodmans was a travel itinerary for a Badgers road football game in 1979, the Big 10 opener against Purdue in West Lafayette. It described lunch at noon at Union South on the Friday before the Sept. 8 game, then a charter flight to Lafayette. On the plane Bob and Irwin sat next to broadcaster Fred Gage and the former Badgers head football coach John Jardine.

Another UW athletics memento saved by Bob and Irwin: A 1997 calendar featuring the great distance runner and Badger star Suzy Favor Hamilton. Suzy personally inscribed a note on the cover:

"To Bob and Irwin,
All my best! Thanks so much for all your support.
You two have been so great over the years!
Thanks!
Your friend,
Suzy Hamilton"

The Goodmans' softball diamond gift was actually the culmination of a process that began in 1991, when the brothers' friend, UW athletic director Pat Richter, made what he called one of the toughest decisions of his career. Facing a nearly $2 million budget deficit and legal pressure to conform to new gender equity requirements in in college athletics, Richter proposed that UW drop several varsity sports. Most of the sports facing the axe were men's. The most controversial was baseball, which had more than 100 years of history on campus. Richter himself had played varsity baseball. The first huge "bonus baby" signed to the pros in the early 1960s was Badgers' outfielder Rick Reichardt, who received $200,000 from the California Angels. There was outrage from some baseball fans in the Madison community, and more tempered anger even from those who sympathized with Richter's position. It was a tough time.

"I had ten guys in my office the other day," Richter told the *Wisconsin State Journal* in March, 1991. "Ten guys I played baseball with, guys who supported baseball. I played the game. It's not easy to get rid of it."

In an interview for this book, Richter said he did not hear from either Bob or Irwin Goodman after making the decision to drop varsity baseball. Certainly the Goodmans had been involved enough in UW athletics, financially and otherwise, that they would have been listened to, but their style had never been to carry a big stick. Richter was grateful, and careful, too, not to draw too heavily on their largesse.

"When I became athletic director," Richter said, "they were, of course, very supportive. I felt like I didn't want to lean on them too hard, because they did so much for so many people."

Even while the varsity baseball program still existed, the Goodmans had expressed an interest in the possibility of UW adding softball as a women's sport. Bob loved the game, and had himself been one of the best ever to play it in Madison.

The brothers spoke to Cheryl Marra, not long after Marra became an associate athletic director for women's sports in 1990.

"When I first met Bob and Irwin Goodman, within two weeks after I got here," Marra recalled, "one of the first things they told me was that they were looking forward to the day when they could contribute to the softball facility." Marra wasn't certain if the Goodmans knew, at the time, that the sport did not yet exist on campus.

In March, 1994, the UW athletic board made the

Irwin and Bob made many friendships in their travels, as people were drawn to their natural friendliness and good will.

decision to add women's softball and women's lacrosse. It brought the number of women's intercollegiate sports to 11, same as the men. It was an effort to comply with new federal legislation requiring gender equity in college athletic programs.

"The addition of women's softball was not a surprise," the *Wisconsin State Journal* reported, "since it is one of the most popular women's collegiate and girls' high school sports. Eleven scholarships will be offered for a roster of 25. The baseball facility will be converted for its use." Competition was slated to begin in 1995–96.

Guy Lohman Field, the baseball facility adjacent to the Nielsen Tennis Stadium on campus, needed work. Richter, and his associate athletic director in charge of softball, Joel Maturi, thought of the Goodmans. Richter had known Bob and Irwin dating to Pat's days as a kid watching Bob play softball for Security State Bank. But in truth, Maturi probably knew them even better.

"Joel was close to them," Richter recalled.

Maturi and his wife, Lois, were friends of the Good-

The theater across State Street from the jewelry store lets Bob know how much he's appreciated.

mans dating back to buying their wedding rings at the State Street store. Joel, at the time, was teaching and coaching at Edgewood High School.

"I don't remember the specifics," Maturi said, "but I wasn't making much money. My first year at Edgewood I made $6,200, teaching and coaching three sports. We got married a short time later. Bob and Irwin set us up with the rings. I think I was paying $25 a month with no interest whatsoever."

From that time on, Maturi, who went on to athletic director positions in Denver and Minnesota after leaving Madison, counted Bob and Irwin as friends.

"They made you feel like you were their best friend," Maturi said, "and that is a unique quality. That's just how they were. They made me feel like a close friend even though deep down I realize they had people who were closer. But it's how they made you feel."

The Maturis went to Brewers games with the brothers—Joel remembered Bob and Irwin packing tofu sandwiches, "a new one on me"—and they went out for meals in Madison, often to Ponderosa.

Even prior to the sport of softball being added in

1994, the brothers had talked to Maturi— who joined the athletic department in 1987—about helping make a softball facility a reality.

"For a couple of years," Maturi said, "we just, I don't want to say joked, but we talked and laughed and it wasn't really serious. But when indeed the university added women's softball, it got serious."

Serious enough that Bob and Irwin invited Richter and Maturi to their Wilson Street home, the apartment building in which they lived in one unit and kept an office in another across the hall. Not a lot of people received invitations to visit the Goodmans at home.

"Joel and I went down to visit them in their apartment on Wilson Street," Richter recalled. "I had never been there before. They lived in one apartment, but everything else was in another apartment. The other apartment was filled with stuff."

Maturi's memories are similar. "Pat and I went up to their apartment," he said. "And from what I understand that was kind of sacred ground. Not a lot of people were invited into the inner sanctum, so to speak, but Pat and I did that. "

Maturi said the brothers were welcoming, but businesslike, too. They discussed UW sports in general, various projects, but, Maturi said, "The thing we kept coming back to was the softball complex."

Maturi continued: "Knowing their passion for the sport itself—Bob had competed in softball in the city for years—it just seemed to make sense. We began to talk about the Goodman Diamond as a good fit for them."

Richter said, "You wouldn't have been disappointed if they had said, 'We'd rather not,' just because of the kind of people they were. In the same vein, we never pushed them. My feeling was, they knew why we were there. We weren't going to try to convince them or dazzle them or anything like that. They knew what they were being asked, and they would either do it or not, and on their terms."

Once it became clear the Goodmans were going to make the lead gift for a new softball complex for UW athletics—Richter and Maturi returned for more meetings over the next several weeks—it was suggested at one point that the Goodman name should be attached to the gift.

"I think Pat deserves credit for that," Maturi said. "I think he—and perhaps Cheryl Marra and myself as well—convinced Bob and Irwin that at this stage of their lives, they need to put their name on something. That was not their modus operandi.

"They gave generously because they thought it was the right thing to do and they had the means to do so. But we felt very strongly they should put their name on this. They needed to be remembered. People needed to know who they were. They wouldn't always be here. We didn't talk in morbid terms, but that was the reality."

Maturi said Bob and Irwin eventually agreed. "They didn't jump at it, by any stretch of the imagination. But they warmed to it as our talks continued."

During those talks in early 1996 Joel Maturi accepted a new job, as athletic director at the University of Denver. On his last official day on the job in Madison, there was one last visit with the Goodmans. On that day, Maturi recalled, he and Richter and Bob and Irwin shook hands on the deal that would have the Goodmans provide a $500,000 lead gift for a UW women's softball facility,

one that would officially be known as the Robert and Irwin Goodman Softball Complex, and, informally, as the Goodman Diamond.

The first person Maturi shared the news with was Karen Gallagher, who had recently been hired as the first women's softball head coach.

"He came up to me," Gallagher recalled later, "all excited, and said, 'I just want to let you know before anybody else that the Goodmans have contributed $500,000 to a new field.'"

That August, prior to a public announcement, Gallagher was introduced to Bob Goodman.

"I didn't know quite what to say to him," Gallagher said. "It's very overwhelming."

The UW made a formal public announcement in October, 1996, at a news conference. Bob attended, Irwin did not. Richter was there, and Gallagher, along with her team, which had debuted, the first women's UW softball team, that spring. At the press conference all the players personally thanked Bob for the brothers' gift.

Bob spoke for himself and Irwin. "Joel Maturi didn't really have to sell us on this wonderful idea as we immediately felt what a terrific addition this would be for the University of Wisconsin athletic program. We truly believe this is a program that is long, long overdue. Its time has come."

The hope was to have the facility—budgeted originally at a total of $1.2 million, it eventually came in at $1.8 million—ready for the 1998 season, but they didn't quite make it. A groundbreaking ceremony was held in late June, 1998. The complex's official address is 2301 University Bay Drive, north of the Nielsen stadium. Bob and Irwin were at the groundbreaking. They wore hardhats and held shovels, as did Richter and Gallagher. The drawings for the facility showed not only a new field but covered grandstands, dugouts and locker rooms, players' lounges, a press box, restrooms and a concession area. The feeling was it should easily become one of a handful of the best women's softball facilities in the country.

Richter introduced Bob and Irwin at the groundbreaking by saying, "I've felt like I've grown up with the Goodmans. From the time I was 8 and 9 years old, I was watching Bob and Irv play softball at Olbrich Park."

UW-Madison Chancellor David Ward spoke and said that the Goodmans' legacy would now include helping grow women's athletics.

Capital Times writer Mike Lucas caught up with Bob and Irwin after the ceremony.

Irwin said, "We believe women's softball will be one of the most watched team sports here at the UW."

Lucas joked to Bob that he looked fit enough to go out and play three innings. "Why would you hold me to only three innings?" Bob said.

Both brothers said they hoped to be at the home opener, the first game in the new facility, in 10 months.

"There was so much more depth to them than I might have guessed," Zaleski said. *"They had traveled the world. They had a life hardly anyone was aware of."*

Early in 1999—with the diamond on pace for a late March opening, a doubleheader against Loyola—coach Karen Gallagher sent the Goodmans a letter and an impressive full color media guide for women's softball, 1999.

"Hello Bob and Irv," Gallagher wrote. "Happy New Year! We are looking forward to a great one. Here is our new media guide, so you get to know some of our new players. I think of both of you often - hopefully we see each other very soon. The field is incredible!"

Irwin, alas, was not able to attend the opener. Bob, who did, said his brother just didn't feel up to it.

The day, March 30, 1999, opened with a reception at the Wisconsin Alumni Research Foundation. Pat Richter, on crutches following hip surgery, welcomed everyone, and introduced Bob Goodman and Chancellor Ward, who made a few remarks.

Then it was over to the new diamond, which sparkled in the sunny, 70-degree weather. Nearly 1,000 fans were in attendance, the largest crowd since the women's soft-

ball program began in 1996. There was a ribbon-cutting ceremony, and after the national anthem was played, Bob Goodman threw out a ceremonial first pitch.

"He was just beaming," Richter said later. "I think he wanted to start playing again."

Bob watched an inning of the game, and then sought out Coach Karen Gallagher to say he was leaving.

"My spirit is with you," Bob said. "But I need to get home to my brother."

Later, *The Capital Times* caught up with Bob at home by telephone. Before the reporter could pose a question, Bob asked, "How are they doing?" (The answer was: They were doing great. The Badgers would sweep Loyola, winning both games of the doubleheader.)

Bob then told *The Capital Times* that Irwin was doing better. "He wanted to be there in the worst way."

Bob also summed up the brothers' feelings about the day. "A dream come true," Bob said. "A moment of being very, very proud."

Coach Gallagher said, speaking of the Goodmans, "They're leaving legacies all over this community because of their generosity."

One of the softball program's first graduates, Carin Bouchard, was in the grandstand as a fan to watch her former team, and said, "It brought tears to my eyes."

Joel Maturi, meanwhile, whose friendship with the Goodmans had helped make the softball diamond a reality, moved from Denver to Minnesota, where he became athletic director of the University of Minnesota. Bob and Irwin made a gift to athletics there in Joel's and Lois's names. Joel said he tracked events in Madison from a distance while the softball facility was being built.

"I continued to follow it," he said, "no question. And when I get back to Madison, which is not as frequently as I would like, quite frankly I drive by the diamond. It gives me a sense of pride and satisfaction. It's a very meaningful thing, and will be forever."

While Bob and Irwin continued to insist, with sincerity, that the softball diamond was not about them, but rather the players and coaches and fans that would benefit from it, they didn't mind the publicity that came with its opening. That was true of other civic projects to which they leant their support, and, in some cases, their names.

Personal publicity, however, was another matter. Bob and Irwin were famously private people. But in the fall of 1993, Bob and Irwin made a rare exception, allowing a lengthy interview in their apartment to *Capital Times* feature columnist Rob Zaleski.

Dave Zweifel, the longtime *Capital Times* reporter and the paper's editor at that point for more than a decade, personally gave Zaleski the assignment: profile Bob and Irwin Goodman. The brothers had just given $100,000 to the United Way for a special fund to help the city's neediest people. It was time for a feature, and Zweifel had a phone number. Zaleski called, and the brothers, with some reluctance, agreed to an interview. Their reluctance, they later confided to Zaleski, wasn't so much talking about their personal lives—although that was surely part of it—but was more that they didn't want people thinking that they were, as Zaleski noted, "seeking headlines." Irwin said he hadn't slept well for a week ahead of the interview.

Yet, once it came to pass, it couldn't have gone better. "Of the couple of thousand interviews I did in my career," Zaleski said, "that one stood out."

Zaleski may have been almost as nervous as the Goodmans. He knew that Bob and Irwin were passionate fans of University of Wisconsin athletics, and Zaleski, before moving to features, had covered the program for almost a decade, first for United Press International, then *The Capital Times*. Zaleski was a good, fair reporter, but unlike some sportswriters in Madison, he never backed away from a controversial story involving Badger sports. He saw it as a part of his job not to back away. As a consequence, he was not universally admired by coaches and administrators. Elroy Hirsch had complained about him to Zweifel. Football coach Dave McClain had stopped speaking to him and basketball coach Bill Cofield had threatened to throw him out of practice.

Zaleski subsequently wondered how he would be received by the Goodmans, who seemed at times to bleed Badger red. He needn't have worried. Not long after they sat down to talk, Zaleski recalled, Bob and Irwin said they had read his sports reporting and did not have a problem with it.

"They respected that I called it as I saw it," Zaleski said.

The Goodmans mentioned that their true favorite among all UW sports was before Zaleski's time. They loved Badger boxing, the sell-out crowds that packed the old Field House. Bob and Irwin said they knew the doomed Badger boxer Charlie Mohr, whose death following a match in April, 1960, led to the sport being abolished. Charlie had stopped in the State Street jewelry store just two days before his fatal bout, to buy a ring for his girlfriend.

"He said it was going to be his last match," Bob said. "He was a beautiful boxer, but he didn't really enjoy fighting. He said he was glad to be through with it."

The talk about sports helped break the ice, Zaleski recalled. He was taken by the modest nature of the brothers' Wilson Street apartment. Rob knew a newspaper journalist, Eldon Knoche, who lived in the building. Bob's and Irwin's unit was very tidy except for a table that was piled with letters, some open and some not. In time, Zaleski would learn what those were about.

He spent, in any case, more than an hour in the apartment. The interview was lengthy, and went well, beginning with the discussion of UW athletics and also the recently defeated attempt by the city in 1993 to build a public pool at Olin Park. Zaleski had written columns in support of the pool project and Bob and Irwin expressed their disappointment that the city had numerous private pools but not one for people without means.

From there, the brothers' talk became wide-ranging: movies, travel, the benefits of a healthy lifestyle, their passion for Madison, their love and respect for each other, even women.

"There was so much more depth to them than I might have guessed," Zaleski said. "They had traveled the world. They had a life hardly anyone was aware of." The brothers said they would be leaving for a cruise to Hong Kong and China just days after the interview.

Bob talked about the closeness of his relationship with Irwin.

"People always say, 'Here come the Bobsey twins.' Or, 'If you see one, you see the other,'" Bob said. "And that's great. One of the things you have to understand—you talk about being successful—one of the main ingredients is the relationship Irv and I have. We're good friends. I have such respect for the man you can't imagine."

Zaleski brought up the subject of the brothers' life-long bachelorhood.

"They were fine talking about it," he recalled. "I think people were afraid to ask. My broaching the subject made them free to talk about it. They were open."

Irwin grinned and said that between them there had been several times over the years when they were close to marriage.

"Speaking for myself," Bob said, "I was always so nuts about sports, always playing ball, 10 days a week. And I'd be dating these girls and I would selfishly feel that they'd love to come out and see me play."

Bob continued, "I really passed up some nice ones. If I had it to do over again, I'd get married, because I love children. But at the time, well . . ."

Zaleski's piece on the Goodmans ran Nov. 19, 1993, in *The Capital Times* under the headline: "Bob, Irv Goodman Add Sparkle to the City."

"They were true originals," Zaleski said, some two decades later, in an interview. "And so genuine. Going into the interview I was thinking that these guys couldn't possibly live up to their image. In fact, they exceeded it."

A lasting image for Zaleski was the letters piled on the dining room table, and at one point Bob and Irwin shared with him that they arrived, unsolicited, almost daily, a dozen or more a month to be certain, mostly from people in need, asking for help.

"They said they picked out a few each month," Zaleski said. "They didn't want any publicity about it."

Of course, not every letter asked for something.

Some just wanted to say thank you. One that must have meant a lot to Bob and Irwin arrived in July, 1997, from Ida Swarsensky, widow of the late, great Rabbi Manfred Swarsensky.

Mrs. Swarsensky enclosed a brief newspaper clipping about the Goodmans being honored for their charitable work and contributions by the United Way of Dane County. Mrs. Swarsensky began:

"Dear Irwin and Bob,
Those of us who are fortunate enough to be numbered among your friends have long been aware that it is people like you who are responsible for the high rating Madison has received as an ideal city."

The letter concluded. . .

"Your philanthropy embraces every human need and much of it is done quietly behind the scenes. May you always be blessed with good health and happiness and may you continue your wonderful work for many years to come.
With respect and admiration,
Ida Swarsensky"

Their philanthropy would continue, but by the time of Mrs. Swarsensky's letter, 1997, Bob and Irwin were giving serious thought to selling the State Street jewelry store that had been a significant part of their lives for 60 years. They had actually been thinking about it since 1995. It would take several years to complete—and it was anything but easy for Bob and Irwin, even though they had a much trusted and admired hand-picked successor—but by 1998, it would happen.

CHAPTER 6
A New Owner for the Store, and New Life for an East Side Community Center

The sale of the jewelry store began, as did so much in the lives of Bob and Irwin, with a Downtown Rotary connection.

The brothers knew a longtime Rotarian, Jon Udell, who was a respected member of the faculty of the UW-Madison School of Business. In the spring of 1995, the Goodmans asked Udell if he would consider helping them sell their jewelry business. The State Street store had been in their family for more than six decades. It was time.

Bob and Irwin knew who they wanted to take over the store. John Hayes had joined them in 1983 and within six months been promoted to sales manager. The brothers liked and trusted Hayes. By 1993, he was the store's general manager, and the Goodmans were comfortable having Hayes occasionally serve as the public face of the business.

In October, 1993, Goodman's Jewelers hosted a three-day exhibition of historic Rolex watches. When the *Wisconsin State Journal* came to write about it, Hayes did the interview, saying "we jumped at the opportunity to be able to show these watches when they were offered to us."

Among the 27 watches on exhibit was one of the first Rolex watches produced by Hans Wilsdorf, the founder of the company, in 1904; the first Rolex from 1931, with a perpetual self-winding timepiece; and a watch with a helium escape valve worn by a scuba diver 4,000 feet under water off Florida in 1987.

Hayes said he particularly liked one that had been worn by Jim Fowler when he hosted the *Wild Kingdom* show on television, a program Hayes especially enjoyed.

It was the kind of thing Bob or Irwin might have said. No surprise, then, that less than two years later, when they approached Udell at Rotary to inquire about help with the sale of the store, the brothers identified Hayes as the one they wanted to buy it.

Udell said he was not equipped to help with the sale, but his office at the business school was next to someone who was—Bob Pricer. Udell gave Bob Goodman Pricer's home phone number.

He called, and Pricer's wife Jane answered. There was some confusion in the first moments of the call. Jane Pricer knew another Bob Goodman at UW-Madison. She and Bob had attended an event at his home.

The Goodmans' association with the store dated to the 1930s, so selling it was not going to be easy.

"Is this the Bob Goodman whose house I was at recently?" Jane said, assuming it must be.

Bob Goodman the jeweler chuckled and said, "No, but I wish it was."

The call began what would become one of the most significant relationships of the last decade of the Goodmans' lives. Within days of the call Bob Pricer visited Bob and Irwin at their Wilson Street apartment. The three of them—life occasionally yields such a gift—hit it off immediately. Pricer and Bob Goodman grew especially close. In their early meetings Irwin's health was not the best—he would later rebound—so Bob was more vocal.

The brothers had insisted early on that Pricer charge his usual consulting fee for his help with the sale. Pricer flatly refused, at first because of his appreciation of the

Goodmans' philanthropy, and later because of his close friendship with them, close enough that they spoke almost daily.

In their first meetings it became clear that Irwin was the one who wanted to sell the store. At the time, his health was declining. He rarely went into the store. Bob, who did walk over to State Street on occasion, was less enthusiastic about selling.

In the end, he deferred to Irwin.

Like so much about Bob and Irwin, their sale of the store would be unique to them. There was no blueprint for what they wanted to do. It was a succession more than a sale, and it was John Hayes they wanted as their successor. To the consternation of their attorneys, who didn't understand, they even let Hayes set the price by asking him what he thought the business was worth. Still, it took a while. As much as they liked Hayes, letting go wasn't easy.

"It was very hard for them," Pricer said. "They vacillated with the conditions of the sale. If it had been anyone else, other than John Hayes, it wouldn't have happened. It was that hard for them."

Hayes agreed. "It was more difficult for Bob than Irwin," he said. "Irwin had been stepping back for some time, coming in maybe a couple of times a week."

Once the Goodmans established an office across the hall from their apartment, Irwin's appearances grew even less frequent. "Only once a month or so," Hayes said. "He was really stepping back. It was harder for Bob. Not so much the business, but people. He liked interacting with people. He thrived on it."

The sale became final in November 1998. And yet even that's a little misleading. You don't just let go of something to which you have given six decades of your life. So while Bob and Irwin rarely came into the store after the sale, they wanted to be kept up to date on its happenings. One component of the sale gave them a large stipend in the event they wanted to buy gifts for friends.

"I would talk to them over the phone," Hayes said. "Or stop up to their office (across from their apartment). We'd go over things and I would keep them up to date about what was going and who was coming in. They were very much interested, but they didn't physically come down."

One exception came several years after the sale when Hayes remodeled the store.

"They came down to see what we had done," Hayes said. "They liked it. We kept the flavor of the store, the wood in the cases. We just brightened it up with new lighting, a new ceiling and some upgrading. They appreciated the changes."

Bob continued to help out with the television ads until at least 2003. A humorous letter in February of that year from a reader to *Capital Times* columnist Bill Dunn posed this question:

"I've noticed the Goodman's Jeweler's ad in which Bob says at the end, 'I'm Bob Goodman. Watch *Friends*. Mr. Goodman doesn't look like the type who'd watch the show. How come that's part of the ad?"

Dunn sought out John Hayes for a reply. Hayes said: "We do sponsor the program on Thursday nights on Channel 27. *Friends* is a program that has a larger audience than one might think. It does attract a younger group than Mr. Goodman in general, but I assure you that he indeed has watched it."

The simple answer is that the Goodmans stayed involved, or at least in touch, because they cared. In 2009, a week after Irwin died, *Wisconsin State Journal* reporter Scott Milfred related a touching story of a call he had received from Irwin, regarding the jewelry business, just a few months earlier.

Milfred had been friendly with the brothers since writing a profile of them in the *State Journal* in 1998. He had been surprised on being given the assignment to find that Bob and Irwin lived in a simple apartment across the

John Hayes has continued to run the jewelry store in the spirit and tradition set by Bob and Irwin.

Bob (left) and Irwin with Wisconsin Gov. Tommy Thompson. The Goodmans helped sponsor Badger State Games.

street from Milfred's own modest digs downtown. They shared a landlord.

After the profile ran, they stayed in touch. Irwin would occasionally call Milfred with a news tip. In March, 2009, he phoned to let Milfred know that John Hayes had recently traveled to Africa to make sure the diamonds Goodman's Jewelers were receiving and selling were obtained in a socially responsible way. The store had helped fund a water treatment plant in South Africa and contributed to a program providing loans to low income women.

Irwin was pleased Hayes was carrying on the Goodman way of doing business. He and Bob would no doubt have also been pleased by a March, 2011, profile of Hayes in the *Wisconsin State Journal* that ran under the headline: "Goodman's Owner Carries on Tradition of Customer Service." And the secondary headline: "Brothers Taught Him Many Valuable Lessons, John Hayes Says."

The last question in the interview was, "What were the main lessons you learned from the Goodmans?"

Hayes replied, "They taught me to treat everybody the way you want to be treated. That was number one, the thing you had to do. On the business side of it, Irwin always said there are three ways to make money: You buy right, sell right, and pay your bills right."

Finally, Hayes got personal. "They never married or had any children and they treated me like a son. I was so lucky. Not a day goes by when I don't want to talk to them or ask them a question."

If, by the 1990s, Bob and Irwin were separating themselves from their jewelry business, they were more engaged than ever with philanthropy.

In 1989, the United Way of Dane County named a new president and chief professional officer. Leslie Ann Howard, who had begun working with a non-profit organization helping the developmentally disabled when she was 14 years old and living in Easton, Pennsylvania, was tapped from an applicant pool of more than 200 from all across the United States. Her father had chaired a United Way campaign in Easton.

Howard earned a master's degree in social work from UW–Madison and within two years, in 1981, she joined the United Way of Dane County as a planning associate and director of the volunteer services bureau.

When she was named president in 1989, Howard was already well acquainted with the Goodmans. "They were around and very supportive," Howard said.

When she got the top job, the relationship grew closer.

"I got a call from Irwin," Howard recalled, "inviting me to their apartment. Irwin said, 'We are going to have a very special relationship.' They wanted to impress upon me that they were very committed to the community, and that we would be actively involved together doing work in the community. That certainly proved to be the case. I don't think they ever said no to me. Anything that we asked for, they found a way to say yes. Which is pretty amazing."

Bob and Irwin had long supported the United Way of Dane County, which took that name in 1971. Prior to that, the organization had been called the United Community Chest, the name chose in 1953 when two groups—the Madison Community Chest and United Givers Fund—merged.

In 1989, the year Leslie Ann Howard was hired as president, the United Way of Dane County received the United Way of America "Second Century Initiative" award for the excellence of its community-wide campaign. The following year, 1990, the United Way started its Tocqueville Society, with membership to those individuals donating $10,000 or more annually.

Bob and Irwin were among six original members, and that, according to Howard, was typical of the brothers' giving.

"They would be on the ground floor," Howard said, "and then what they liked to do was stimulate others to step up. When I would sit down with them each year to talk about their gift for the following year, Irwin would always say, 'Who gives the next highest?' They liked being the highest, and they wanted to stay there, but they wanted other people coming along with them as well."

"They didn't really want a lot of recognition," Howard continued. "If they did want it, it was more as a way to stimulate others to give. 'We're at this level, now other people should be at this level.'"

Over time Howard developed a personal relationship and friendship with the Goodmans.

"They gave through relationships," she said. "That meant a lot to them and I think as they got older it meant even more."

The brothers would call and suggest a movie. Their taste was wide-ranging. Howard recalled seeing her first Adam Sandler comedy—*The Waterboy*—with Bob and Irwin. Another time they wanted to see a British import, *Calendar Girls,* about some older women who decide to raise money by posing for sexy calendar photos. Howard chuckled when recalling that shortly before she left to pick the brothers up for that one, her phone rang. It was Irwin.

"Are you sure it's OK for you to come to this movie?" Irwin said. "It's a little racy."

Howard would cook dinner—vegetarian, of course—for the brothers in her home and accompany them for meals at favored restaurants like Ponderosa and Himal Chuli on State Street.

"We talked about relationships," Howard recalled. "Girlfriends. . . Bob did say a couple of times to me that if he had one regret it was that he didn't take the time to have a longstanding relationship, and a marriage. That was interesting. But they were so busy with their business and their charity and all their other pursuits."

Howard continued, "They really loved Madison. Whenever we got a new mayor or a new county executive, they would say, 'What do you think of them? How are they going to do for the city?'"

In March, 1993, the United Way of Dane County announced the formation of the United Way Foundation. The Goodmans were among the original five donors who helped establish the foundation, which differs from ongoing fund drives in that donations to a foundation are generally invested rather than immediately distributed.

In May, 1993, two months after the announcement of the United Way Foundation, Bob and Irwin pledged $100,000 to establish a separate fund inside the foundation.

Irwin told the *Wisconsin State Journal* the money would be used to "provide for the emergency and ongoing needs of individuals and families who lack minimal basic material resources for food and shelter; for the physical, emotional and crisis needs of children; and to provide opportunities for the elderly to remain independent."

Oscar Mayer executive Jerry Hiegel, chairman of the foundation, said "the Goodmans came to us and we have worked very closely with them to develop this fund in a way that would provide those kinds of services and programs to the people who need this help the most desperately."

"Their great concern was poor children," Howard said, "Children who are in poverty or who are homeless."

Howard continued, "When they established what they wanted their funds at the foundation to go for, it was really focused on children, low income children, children with food and shelter needs. That really concerned them. That we could be in a place like Madison, but there were still these problems and needs."

Howard recalled a time when her conversation with Bob and Irwin turned to the city's at risk neighborhoods. There was one in particular, she said, that lacked even a playground for the neighborhood children.

"Maybe two days later I got a call," Howard said. It was the Goodmans. "We want to put a playground in there," they said. "What do we have to do?"

Howard recalled, "They built a playground."

In 1995, Madison Mayor Paul Soglin helped the United Way initiate "Goodman Day" in the city, celebrated annually around the brothers' birthdays (Bob was June 28; Irwin July 1).

Kathy Hubbard is a longtime United Way of Dane County employee, who, like Howard, became close to Irwin and Bob. Hubbard recalled that an early "Goodman Day" celebration coincided with the opening of a playground sponsored by the brothers. "We started with big celebrations," Hubbard recalled, "but they didn't really like big celebrations. We thought it would be great, but they were very low key, and then the sun became an issue. They didn't want to come out in the sun. I'll never forget they funded a playground at Vera Court, and we had a celebration at the playground that they were there

Hubbard recalled that when her mother died, the Goodmans found out and insisted on making a $5,000 contribution in her honor to the United Way Foundation.

for. We always had shade for them. They loved the idea of helping children with physical activity. They supported the playground at the Boys and Girls Club. They wanted to make sure kids were physically active."

The year of the first "Goodman Day," 1995, was the year Hubbard, whose United Way service now spans more than three decades, took on a special role with the Goodmans, helping them process the myriad of requests they received for financial help.

"Leslie had a meeting with them," Hubbard recalled. "And at that time Bob and Irwin were saying how confusing it was getting with all the requests. They were inundated. At that time I had been with the organization

about 13 years, and I had a pretty good knowledge of the non-profits in the community. Leslie offered my services to them to help them cull through the requests and make recommendations."

It proved, for Hubbard, a rewarding experience.

"I found them both to be amazing gentlemen," she said. "I grew up without a grandfather so I immediately sort of adopted them. And they took a real interest in me—in all of us who worked with them. They knew about my family, they watched my son grow up."

Looking back and appraising her role with the Goodmans, Hubbard said,

"In some ways, it was to help Irwin say no. He had trouble with that. I would go and they would have stacks of things for me to take. I would take them back, go through them all, and make up charts showing what the agencies were, what they were asking for, how much money they wanted, and whether it was personal or a regular ask. I would bring them back to them and we would literally go over them one by one.

It was fascinating. They cared so much. It was so hard—especially for Irwin—to say no to anyone. We started to talk about their personal interests and maybe focusing their 'yeses' on those. And over time they did that, and we tried to make sure that in making decisions, it was the right thing for them, in the sense of their beliefs and their values. And they would want to know about a group's finances, its motives, and if anyone else was supporting it. They had to be strategic in what they supported. But they felt so blessed, and they wanted to make sure this community had what it needed."

Hubbard recalled lunches at Ponderosa, occasions when she was in their apartment, and times when Bob and Irwin asked if she might drive them on an errand. She took them to buy avocados and to a health food store on Monroe Street.

"They knew where things were on sale," she said, "and where the deals were. They were extremely frugal."

With themselves they were frugal. Hubbard recalled

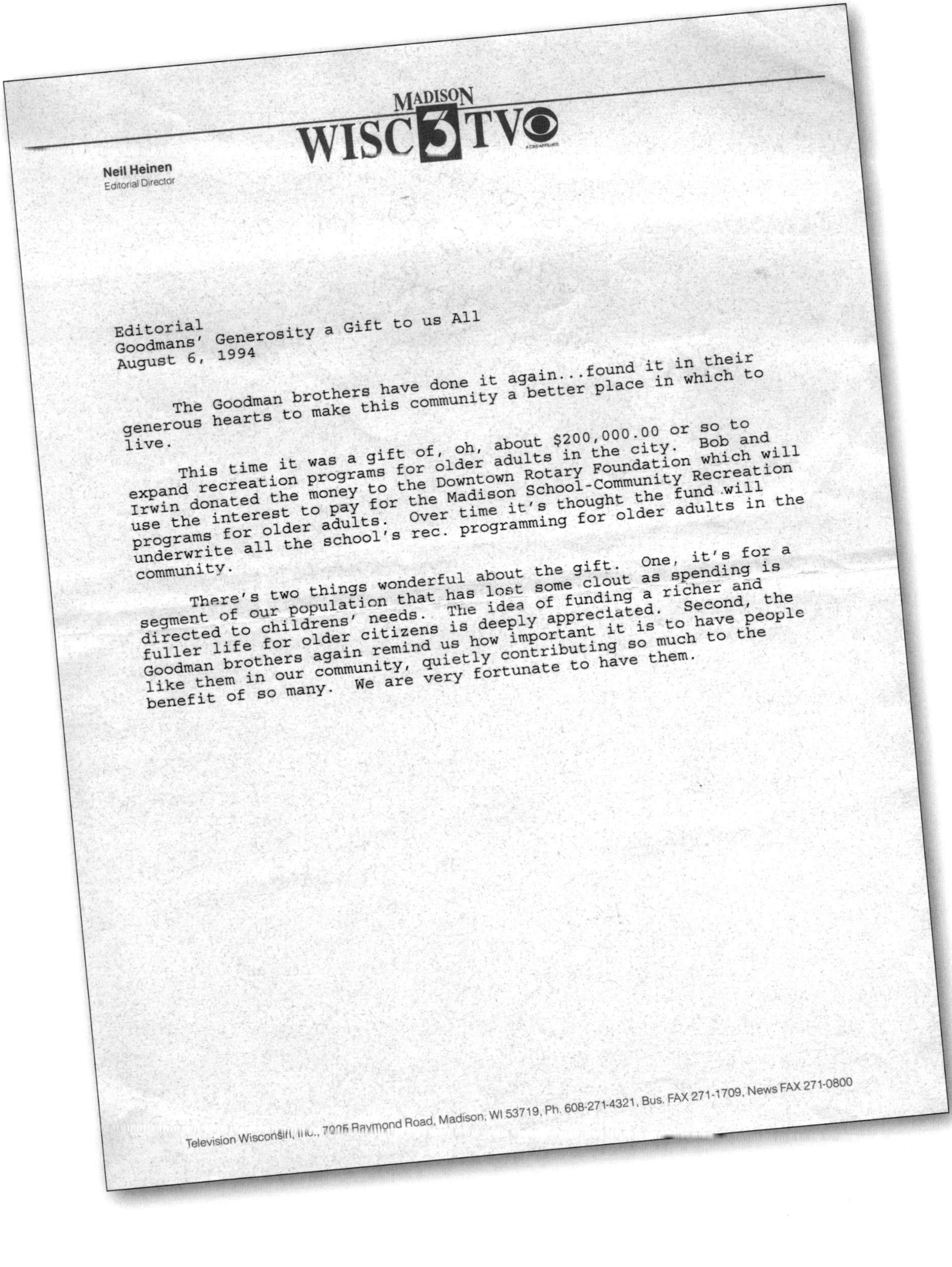

MADISON
WISC 3 TV

Neil Heinen
Editorial Director

Editorial
Goodmans' Generosity a Gift to us All
August 6, 1994

The Goodman brothers have done it again...found it in their
generous hearts to make this community a better place in which to
live.

This time it was a gift of, oh, about $200,000.00 or so to
expand recreation programs for older adults in the city. Bob and
Irwin donated the money to the Downtown Rotary Foundation which will
use the interest to pay for the Madison School-Community Recreation
programs for older adults. Over time it's thought the fund will
underwrite all the school's rec. programming for older adults in the
community.

There's two things wonderful about the gift. One, it's for a
segment of our population that has lost some clout as spending is
directed to childrens' needs. The idea of funding a richer and
fuller life for older citizens is deeply appreciated. Second, the
Goodman brothers again remind us how important it is to have people
like them in our community, quietly contributing so much to the
benefit of so many. We are very fortunate to have them.

Television Wisconsin, Inc., 7025 Raymond Road, Madison, WI 53719, Ph. 608-271-4321, Bus. FAX 271-1709, News FAX 271-0800

Channel 3 editorial director
Neil Heinen was among
many who admired the
Goodmans, and said so in
this transcript of an editorial.

that when her mother died, the Goodmans found out and insisted on making a $5,000 contribution in her honor to the United Way Foundation.

"It was so touching to me," Hubbard said. "That's how they were. They did that all the time."

Like many in Bob and Irwin's orbit, Hubbard marveled at the closeness of their relationship. Bob would often defer to Irwin. If she visited when Irwin's health wasn't the best, the first thing Bob would say was, "Doesn't Irwin look great today?"

"I've never seen a love between two brothers like it," Hubbard said.

Her United Way colleague Leslie Ann Howard witnessed the same thing.

"There was a great deal of caring between the two of them that became even more apparent toward the end, when Bob was caring for Irwin," Howard said. "Irwin—like

Today the United Way of Dane County has an annual award – the Goodman Gemstone of Youth Award – that honors young people for community service.

a lot of us—would worry a lot. People asked him for things. He always wanted to say yes and of course he couldn't. So he worried and Bob would try to protect him."

There came a point when Bob's health declined, and Irwin, though not well, willed himself back to the fore.

"Irwin stepped up," Howard said. "I was thinking, 'Wow. Does that show love?' Even though Irwin was frail, he pushed himself back out in front."

Over the years the United Way tried to honor the Goodmans in a public way when possible—when Bob and Irwin would allow it—with the "Goodman Day" celebration being a prime example.

"Goodman Day" 1997 was July 1, Irwin's 82nd birthday. The United Way hosted a gathering at the Kennedy Heights Community Center to salute Bob and Irwin's recent gift of a refrigerated truck to the Commu-

nity Action Coalition of South Central Wisconsin. The truck would deliver fresh food to the coalition's 31 food pantries around the county. The next day, the *Wisconsin State Journal* ran an editorial that noted the following: "In truth, every day in Madison and Dane County is 'Goodman Day' because they care so much about the city and Dane County. One day has been set aside to honor their generosity, but their gifts pay community dividends 365 days a year."

At the end of 1997, it developed that the United Way of Dane County was going to fall short of its fund-raising goal of $9.3 million.

"I don't remember the exact amount but we were significantly short of our goal," Leslie Ann Howard recalled. "It was a tough year for the economy. They would always ask if we were going to meet our goal. I had to say I didn't think so. So they stepped up, and challenged other people, who came on board, and we met our goal that year."

The Goodmans had been planning a $100,000 United Way donation, a figure they increased by $80,000 upon hearing of the shortfall.

"They really appreciated that we asked them," Kathy Hubbard said, "and that they could come in and support the campaign that way."

Campaign chair Hal Mayer wrote a letter to *The Capital Times* calling the Goodmans' $180,000 donation "by far the largest individual pledge received in any United Way of Dane County campaign."

There was a similar circumstance a few years later, following the terrorist attacks in September 2001, when it appeared United Way of Dane County might fall short of its ($13.34 million) goal for the year. Bob and Irwin came through with $200,000.

"They would not let us fail," campaign chair Bill Harvey told *The Capital Times*.

In between those two potential shortfalls for the organization, in 1999–2000, Bob and Irwin donated $100,000 to a capital campaign for a new United Way of Dane County building. The Atwood Avenue facility has a conference room named for the Goodmans.

Today the United Way of Dane County has an annual award—named the Goodman Gemstone of Youth Award—

Madison Mayor Paul Soglin speaking at a State Street ceremony honoring Bob and Irwin.

that honors young people for community service.

"They always worried if there would be people to pick up the slack," Kathy Hubbard said, "to step forward after they were gone. This was such a huge part of their lives."

In reflecting on Bob and Irwin's long relationship with United Way, Howard said, "They kind of set the vanguard in terms of how far people should go, how far people should stretch, how much can we accomplish? When others would sit back, they would come in. And that was huge because of the relationships they had built up in the community. They had such credibility and because they believed in us and supported us, others did too. That meant everything."

Howard, who grew close enough to the brothers that Bob, after Irwin's death, asked her (in the Jewish tradition) to leave a stone next to Irwin's grave every day for

three months, recalled how in their last years the Goodmans became a bit more receptive to making "naming" gifts and having their philanthropy recognized by the public.

"They did talk about creating a foundation and a legacy with their funds," Howard said, "but I remember Irwin saying they also wanted to enjoy some of it while they were still here. I saw a big shift at that time, maybe five years or so before they were gone.

"They started doing some bigger things," Howard continued. "It made a lot of sense. Obviously their foundation was going to be big. But do some things that make it clear what you're interested in, and let the community see that. So they stepped up and did some bigger things—with their names attached—and that was the point, too, when they kind of realized their mortality, and thought, 'Let's enjoy

Some consider the Goodman Community Center, located on Madison's east side, to be the Goodmans' most significant gift.

some of this while we're still here.' I think they got a real satisfaction out of knowing they were helping."

The Goodmans' last big naming gift during their lifetimes—a gift that some in the community, including some of Bob and Irwin's close friends, feel is their most important—would be seen by some as a departure. The brothers had always supported physical fitness, nutrition, athletics, Jewish causes, but their major gift to the Atwood Community Center—which became the Goodman Community Center—on Madison's east side was directed at helping the city's vulnerable populations, young and old. It would not be difficult to argue that the gift was not so unusual. Bob and Irwin had always been quick to help seniors, and kids, too, through their various United Way donations.

The Atwood Community Center had a history dating

back to 1954. The building itself, at 2425 Atwood Avenue, went back much further. It was built originally in 1917 as a hotel where men working at the nearby Madison Kipp factory could stay. In 1925 it became home to the East Side Businessmen's Club. When that club relocated to its current home on Lake Monona, not far from Olbrich Park, they donated the building to the United Community Chest, the forerunner of United Way, which had established an umbrella group titled United Neighborhood Centers. The facility at 2425 Atwood Avenue became one. In 1954, the Atwood property officially became the Atwood Community House, a name that would eventually be changed to the Atwood Community Center.

Early on, according to newspaper accounts from that time, the Atwood Community House focused on assisting what *The Capital Times* called, in a 1969 story, "social dropouts and the delinquents."

When a new director, Paul Koeshall, took over in 1966, he moved to expand the reach of the center, to make it a true gathering place for the Atwood community. Koeshall and his assistant director, Barbara Olson, met with neighborhood groups and individuals to both explain their plan and get input.

"We thought a community center should be open to all people," Olson told *The Capital Times*. Koeshall explained it in a little more depth: "We feel that we can help the child who is having some social, emotional or interpersonal problem even more effectively in a group that isn't exclusively full of 'problem children,'" Koeshall said.

Koeshall continued, "It is our philosophy that kids learn best from other kids in small friendship groups where there is a cross section of racial, economic and personal society."

Although school kids remained the focus, there were also—and this would presage the center's mission more than four decades later—programs for seniors, preschoolers and the entire neighborhood population.

If that broadening of scope was a milestone in the growth of the Atwood Community Center, another came in 1988, when a young woman named Becky Steinhoff joined the center as a social work intern.

Steinhoff grew up in the Hyde Park neighborhood of

When Bob and Irwin's $2 million gift to the Community Center was announced, a *Capital Times* headline read: "Goodman Brothers Do It Again."

Chicago, and came to Madison to attend the University of Wisconsin in 1984. She was studying social work and psychology, and had a deep interest in community organizing.

In 1988, as part of her internship at the Atwood Community Center, Steinhoff held a series of neighborhood meetings to see what residents thought could be improved. The recycling of bottles and cans and paper kept coming up. There was no curbside recycling in 1988. People who saw it as good for the neighborhood and environment had to drive their recyclables to a center on Fish Hatchery Road.

Steinhoff organized a volunteer-run recycling program through the Atwood Community Center. Volunteers drove donated trucks around the neighborhood and picked up the clear bags filled with recyclable material left by residents at the curb. The program was a great success. Later, the city of Madison would adopt the clear bag program, and an early Atwood volunteer, George

Dreckmann, would become the longtime director of Madison's recycling program.

Becky Steinhoff became executive director of the Atwood Community Center in 1991. Her energy and vision increased the center's profile, but that brought associated challenges. As the center continued to grow, with more programs and more participants, the center was forced to buy or rent space in other locations.

In 2004, the Atwood Community Center celebrated its 50th anniversary. There was a large party at the nearby Olbrich Botanical Gardens. Hundreds attended, the event was sold out. There was a catered dinner and birthday cake, with the dining room filled with balloons, along with paintings and murals created by the kids in the Center's after school programs. "Known for its extensive programming and involved community," *The Madison Times* reported in an article on the anniversary, "Atwood Community Center provides everything from a food pantry to youth and senior programming."

Becky Steinhoff told the *Wisconsin State Journal*: "When I first started here, we had one elementary after-school program and a senior program that met a couple of times a week. Now we have 200 or more kids a day in seven different programs. We operate out of four buildings."

The scattered locations were clearly not ideal for the Atwood Community Center. Around the time of the 50th anniversary, Becky Steinhoff said, "Consolidating under one roof came up."

The center hired consultants and four sites in the Atwood neighborhood were considered. In neighborhood

"Never doubt that a small group of thoughtful, committed citizens can change the world. Indeed, it's the only thing that ever has." —Margaret Mead

focus groups, an abandoned ironworks building at 149 Waubesa Street kept coming up. It offered abundant space, and the building in its present state was an eyesore. It had originally been Kupfer Ironworks. The most recent inhabitant had been Durline Scales, a manufacturer of truck scales. The company had struggled and not done much in the way of maintenance.

"We started looking at it," Steinhoff said, of the building at 149 Waubesa Street. "I was skeptical to say the least."

She found the claims that Durline had deferred maintenance on the building to be an understatement. "They were on the way out when they came here and probably did more harm than good," Steinhoff said. When it rained it could fill with half a foot of water. One of the factory workers told Steinhoff, "Oh, yeah, we'd just put on our galoshes and keep working. It always leaked."

For all that, under its exterior was a beautiful brick building with 300 windows, the site was perfect, the amount of space—44,000 feet—enviable. Steinhoff and her board decided to try to purchase it. An anonymous

donor came forward with $300,000 to seed the campaign to fund the relocation.

The first public notice was a *Wisconsin State Journal* story in June, 2005. It was a complicated deal involving tax credits. Fundraising began in earnest that summer. As Steinhoff recalled, the campaign started strong, but as often happens with major projects, after the initial excitement, donations dropped off. By mid-2006, Atwood needed a major donor who could reinvigorate the campaign.

It was then that a woman named Doris Hanson, who had served on the Atwood Community Center Board, and was on the capital campaign committee, suggested approaching Bob and Irwin Goodman.

"Doris was a friend of Bob's particularly," Steinhoff said. "She was quite the softball player, and had played softball with Bob."

In fact, Bob Goodman had coached a women's softball team for which Doris Hanson played shortstop. Women's athletics was just one cause dear to Hanson's heart. She was an extraordinary public servant in Wisconsin. Hanson served in the state Legislature and in the cabinets of four governors, including secretary of the Department of Administration, appointed by Tony Earl. She was a trailblazer for the rights of women in the work place and on the athletic field. In the Legislature, Hanson championed what was called "comparable worth" legislation for women. She also served as president of the WIS (Women's Intercollegiate Sports) Club, which promoted equal opportunity for female athletes.

One day in 2006, Doris Hanson called her old friend Bob Goodman to talk about the Atwood Community Center. It was the beginning of a long road that would end with a gift some feel is the Goodmans' most significant. It shouldn't be surprising that it took a while. The amount being discussed was large. Bob and Irwin, originally, did not know a lot about the center. People were always approaching them. Even when that person was as good a friend and as respected a citizen as Doris Hanson, they were leery.

"Doris convinced them to spend some time getting to know the organization before they answered," Steinhoff said. "I think they agreed as a favor to Doris, not really intending to make the gift."

Bob and Irwin asked a trusted friend, Bob Pricer, who had helped them with the sale of the jewelry business, to take a close look at the Atwood Community Center and report back.

"I started to look at the program," Pricer said, "and the more I looked into the Atwood Community Center, the more I understood that this was a phenomenal place. I started to go back to Bob and Irwin, bringing materials back, making charts, and I said, 'This is something you should really, really look into.'"

Pricer himself is not easily impressed, but the Atwood Community Center impressed him. He said: "Who they served, the numbers they served, and the range of people—everyone from preschool to seniors. Becky Steinhoff is a visionary and a force of nature. I don't think people really appreciate how good Becky is. She gets things done. I interviewed people who used the services. One of Irwin's caretakers had a family member who had children in a preschool program. I couldn't find anyone associated with that center who felt it hadn't made a difference in their lives."

Eventually Bob and Irwin were impressed, too. "They really liked Becky," Pricer said. "Irwin was a good judge of people. He appreciated the programs. We literally went through every program that the center had, the printed information, he saw it all. "

Doris Hanson was thrilled when the agreement with Bob and Irwin was reached. Becky Steinhoff's recollection is that Doris brought their letter of commitment into her office—along with the memorable instructions, "don't screw this up"—and then spent a busy election day, Nov. 6, 2006, doing among other things a radio interview. Doris Hanson died that night, at 81.

The agreement was that for the Goodmans' $2 million donation, the center would be renamed the Irwin A. and Robert D. Goodman Community Center. The center board had struggled with that a bit, but in the end they were grateful. There were donors they had courted who came in after Bob and Irwin's gift was publicized.

"It wasn't about putting their names on things,"

Steinhoff said. "It had nothing to do with ego. These were two amazingly humble, wonderful guys. It had everything to do with making a mark in a city they loved."

When the $2 million gift was first announced to the public, it received abundant news coverage. *The Capital Times* front page headline on March 5, 2007, read: "Goodman Brothers Do It Again."

Becky Steinhoff was quoted: "We are thrilled. The Goodmans stand for a lot in this community, and we are very proud of our association with them and very touched by this."

Bob and Irwin did not attend the press conference announcing the gift, though they issued a statement: "We are impressed by the programs and services provided by the Atwood Community Center. It is a privilege to be members of this very special community and we are thankful that we have the opportunity to both live in Madison and to be able to support a better future for all of our community.'

Bob and Irwin became good friends with Becky Steinhoff. They invited her to join Downtown Rotary.

"I resisted," she said. "But I did it for Irwin. I'm still there. I enjoy it very much."

In the months leading up to the grand opening of the new center—in September 2008—Steinhoff kept the brothers posted on its progress.

"They came out and went through the building three or four times," she said. "The first time it was the middle of construction, messy, dusty, and Irwin was in a wheelchair. But it was OK.

"I sent them photos and budgets," Steinhoff continued. "Irwin called me a lot. I would say he probably called once a week to chat. Sometimes it was something about the building, and sometimes it was just to chat. I remember once I was in New York City on the bus when he called. He thought that was pretty wild—that he reached me on my cell phone on a bus in New York City."

Five years on, Steinhoff is pleased and proud of the progress the center has made, and ever grateful for the Goodmans' generosity.

"I think in some ways this was a different kind of investment for them," she said. "They were very focused on health and fitness, being active, and eating healthy. This was perhaps their first investment in a project that targeted in its programs lower income people. We had great conversations about the challenges Madison faced, which were a lot different at the end of their lives from when they first came here."

In fact, 70 years had passed since they'd established themselves in Madison. Steinhoff recalled one visit in particular that Bob and Irwin made to the center.

"They liked to come when the building was really quiet," she said. "They didn't like a lot of attention. But they came in once when programming was going on and the kids came up and met them. Irwin loved that."

He and Bob would no doubt also appreciate a line from the anthropologist Margaret Mead that has long been embraced by the Goodman Community Center: "Never doubt that a small group of thoughtful, committed citizens can change the world. Indeed, it's the only thing that ever has."

CHAPTER 7
A Lasting Legacy

In their later years, when Bob and Irwin could not get out as much as they liked, good friends would come to them.

"The last three or four years of their lives," Mary Rouse said, "I would visit at their apartment every two or three weeks. I'd take flowers and fresh fruit juice. They always wanted to hear about what was going on."

Rouse considered herself privileged to be a friend of the Goodmans. In a piece she wrote for the Jewish Social Services newsletter, *Connections*, she crafted this lovely sentence about Bob and Irwin: "They treated their friends as if they were amazing and special gifts."

Rouse first met the Goodmans in the 1970s. She worked on the UW–Madison campus across four decades, starting in undergraduate admissions in the late 1960s. She spent a dozen years as dean of students, beginning in 1987, and in 1999, left that position to be assistant vice chancellor for academic affairs. At the same time Rouse became head of the Morgridge Center for Public Service on campus, which matches students with volunteer activities.

"I felt this is where my heart and mind are at this time," Rouse told the *Wisconsin State Journal*, adding, with a touch of humor, "I've been a community servant myself since my hair was black."

One might guess that a shared interest in community service is what first drew Rouse together with Bob and Irwin. In fact, it was their diets. One year in the 1970s, Rouse agreed to run the year-end banquet for the UW track and field and cross country teams. The Winged Foot booster club sponsored the event. Bob and Irwin, unsurprisingly, were members, though they had never attended the banquet. As a part of her duties, Rouse set the menu for the banquet. She is not a big meat eater, and she added a vegetarian option. It brought a call from Bob Goodman.

"He said, 'We're coming to the banquet,'" Rouse recalled. "And then he said, 'We'd like to know who put the vegetarian entrée on the menu. We're vegetarians.'"

Rouse replied, "It was me," and introduced herself. Bob said, "We'd like to meet you," and that happened, at the banquet. Subsequently they would chat in the press box on football Saturdays at Camp Randall, or at Rotary, and Rouse gained an appreciation of the brothers' true character.

"I had seen them on their television commercials in their polyester suits," she said. "I honestly thought they were a little goofy. Once I got to know them, I saw how

Irwin Goodman drives an ancient Olds, but gives generously to charitable causes.
—*State Journal photo by A. Craig Benson*

This *Wisconsin State Journal* clipping references how Bob and Irwin lived modestly, despite their wealth.

warm, positive and affirmative they were."

Like so many others, Rouse would find herself swept up in their cheerful warmth.

"They could always find something positive to say about somebody, or about something that was going on," she said. "They did not operate in the negative realm of this world. They just did not."

The friendship grew closer. "We bonded," Rouse said. Bob and Irwin invited Mary, her husband and their son to sit in their box behind home plate at Brewers game in Milwaukee. They had boxes of fruit delivered to her front door. They gave her a watch that she still wears and over the years made her the gift of several clocks.

"I think they forgot how many they gave me," Rouse said. Bob would occasionally call.

"Are you using our clock?"

"Of course I am."

"What time is it?"

Or Bob might tell one of his "groaner" jokes. Rouse

recalled one she heard more than once. It involved two guys on a golf course who while they're playing observe a funeral procession go by on a street adjacent to the course.

One of the golfers stops and puts his cap over his heart.

"Why are you doing that?" the second golfer asks.

"She was a good wife."

Like nearly everyone in the Goodmans' circle, Rouse was impressed by their modest lifestyle and quiet philanthropy. She coined a term for them: communitarians, "rare individuals whose allegiance is to the greater good of the community."

It seems of a part with their great capacity for friendship.

"They treated me like I was a gift to them," Rouse said. "The real gift was to me, to know them as long as I did, and to get to spend as much time with them as I did."

Bob and Irwin continued close relationships even with those friends who moved from the Madison area. Maybe they couldn't see each other as much as they once had, but they stayed in touch, and more. Certainly that was the case with Russ Hellickson and his wife, Nancy, after they left Madison for Columbus, Ohio, in 1986, when Russ became head wrestling coach at Ohio State University.

Russ and Nancy both came out of Stoughton High School, and like so many young couples in and around Madison, they got their engagement ring at Goodman's on State Street. Russ bought it on a layaway plan. More than 40 years later, he'd remember paying $10 a month.

There came a time, the Christmas season of 1968, when Russ couldn't make that month's payment. He was a student at UW–Madison, playing sports, and had spent the little extra money he had on holiday gifts. One evening he went to the store to speak to the Goodmans. Nancy waited across the street. It was a cold December night and she could look in the jewelry store's window and see Bob smiling and talking to Russ.

"I told him I didn't think that I could make that month's payment," Russ recalled. "I said it might be a month or two more before I could. Bob said, 'Well, how much money do you need?'"

Hellickson was astonished. Not only was Bob not asking for that month's payment, he was offering money of his own to help in a tough time.

"He gave me money," Hellickson recalled, wonder still in his voice some 45 years later. "He may have added it to my bill, I'm not certain. He may well not have. But I'll never forget that he took out his wallet and handed me cash. Fifty or one hundred dollars. I got emotional. I thanked him. He said, 'You're not just my customer, you're my friend.' I went three or four months without paying, and then I was able to come in and start paying again."

Russ and Nancy got married in July 1970. They invited Bob and Irwin and were delighted the brothers accepted the invitation.

"They came to the church and they came to the reception," Nancy said. "It was so touching that they did that. I felt so special."

Russ had played football for the Badgers, lettering in his sophomore year, but soon decided that his best sport was wrestling. "Bob encouraged me," Russ said.

Hellickson made the United States team for the Pan American Games in 1971. The Pan Am Games are an international competition held in the year proceeding Olympic years. That year they were held in Colombia. Russ went down ahead of Nancy and it turned out that when Nancy did come, Bob and Irwin were on the flight. They were affiliated with the United States Olympic Committee through boxing and were going to the Pan Am Games in South America in some sort of official capacity.

"They told me not to worry, they would take care of Nancy," Russ said. They not only did that, they arranged for the Hellicksons to get a good deal on South American emeralds.

"They were the most generous people I ever met in my life," Russ said.

In 1972, Russ started a wrestling newspaper, the *Crossface,* and Goodman's Jewelers was one of the first advertisers. Any way they could help, they did. Years later, Hellickson, who would become wrestling coach at UW, wrote Bob Goodman a note recalling their largesse.

"You and Irwin never hesitated to support any and all Wisconsin wrestling activities I brought before you,"

Hellickson wrote. "We are always indebted to you and Irwin for your generous contributions, your support of the programs for the [wrestling] meets, yearbooks, my television show *Crossface,* the Soviet duals, and other international events. I never took your support for granted, but in my heart I knew I could always rely on the two of you to help make my wrestling interests flourish. Not many people can say they have friends like that."

Bob and Irwin were on the flight. They were affiliated with the United States Olympic Committee through boxing and were going to the Pan Am Games in some sort of official capacity.

After Hellickson won a silver medal in the 1976 Olympics, he underwent neck surgery, and Bob and Irwin visited him in the hospital in Madison. It was a Sunday afternoon. Nancy recalled that she was sitting and chatting with her husband when the brothers came in. After being assured that Russ was doing well, Irwin turned to Nancy—she would be far from the only woman to get this advice from Irwin—and suggested she uncross her legs because crossing them was bad for the blood flow in her veins. Decades later, Nancy laughed and said, "To this day I'll be sitting somewhere and I'll cross my legs and hear Irwin telling me not to."

In 1986, Russ and Nancy moved to Columbus, Ohio, and Russ became wrestling coach at Ohio State University. There was no question of Bob and Irwin not maintaining the friendships. "They called and wrote letters," Nancy said. "They were woven into the fabric of our lives."

She kept a card that arrived in Columbus one year at the holidays. It was in Bob's handwriting.

"Dear Nancy and Russ,
We do hope the two nicest people we know are enjoying good health. If we wrote to you every time we thought of you, you would have no room in your house. Russ you are so lucky to have so many wonderful women in your household and Nancy you are

married to one of the most respected men anywhere. Boy how we wish you lived in Madison.

                                        Love, Irwin and Bob"

On the Hellicksons' 30th wedding anniversary, in 2000, Bob helped Russ pick out a diamond ring for Nancy. John Hayes had purchased the store by then but Bob told Russ, "You tell me when you're going to be here and I'll meet you at the store."

Around that time—the early 2000s—it was clear from the brothers' phone calls and letters that life was becoming more difficult. One time Bob was on the line and

The scope of their giving was already remarkable, but the decade following that article's publication would bring even more generous gifts, the most significant of the Goodmans' lives.

said they just couldn't do all the things they wished they could. They missed some of what they had done in the past, especially activities they did together.

"We don't buy green bananas anymore," Bob said. But it was all right, he added. "It's OK for us to slow down. We don't have anything to prove."

During one of those phone calls the Goodmans first broached the idea for a gift that became a reality in 2004. They wanted to honor Russ's years of coaching, and the Buckeye wrestling program was moving into a new facility. What about a wall that would depict life-size figures of the Buckeyes' national champion wrestlers? Bob and Irwin made a $30,000 donation, and the wall includes a plaque with this inscription:

> "This NCAA Championship Wall is maintained through a generous endowment given in honor of Russ and Nancy Hellickson by their good friends, Bob and Irwin Goodman, May, 2004."

Russ was deeply appreciative. "If you go into the wres-

tling facility, you would have no idea I coached 20 years at Ohio State, except for that plaque on the wall."

One of the last notes to Columbus arrived in January, 2009.

> "Thank you for your wonderful Christmas card with the picture of your beautiful family. We are sure your children and grandchildren add real meaning to your life. We really enjoyed your visit this past year and wish we were able to come see you as well. However, given our ages, we stay close to home, but keep our interest in sporting events, especially those involving the Badgers. We have such fond memories of you and think of you often. We want you to know how much we appreciate hearing from you. Your card with the picture of your family really brightened our day."

The curtain was descending. Some months later, on a visit to the Goodmans' apartment, their great friend from the UW, Mary Rouse, told Bob and Irwin that three generations of her family would be bicycling in the first ever "Ride the Drive" event in downtown Madison. Rouse took out a map and showed the brothers that the route took riders onto John Nolen Drive, where Bob and Irwin could see them from their balcony.

The first "Ride the Drive" was August 29, 2009. "I had been telling them all summer about the event and encouraging them to watch it," Rouse wrote later of the Goodmans. "As fitness buffs and sports enthusiasts, they were very excited."

On the big day, three generations of Rouses—aged 4 to 71—rode together in the event and stopped their bicycles below the Goodmans' apartment.

"Irwin came out and waved," Rouse recalled. "He had a broad and serene smile as he greeted us from their third floor balcony. "

Rouse called up, "Goodbye! I love you and I'll be by to see you in a few days."

The next day, August 30, 2009, Irwin Goodman died. He was 94.

Irwin's death was front-page news in the *Wisconsin*

State Journal on Sept. 1, 2009. The news story was written by Matthew DeFour and William Wineke, and began: "Irwin Goodman, a pillar of the Madison community who along with his brother, Robert, gave more than $10 million to philanthropic causes, died Sunday at his Madison home."

The story quoted United Way president Leslie Ann Howard: "Irwin put most of his means toward the community, rather than his own life. The community really was his child."

Mayor Dave Cieslewicz was interviewed and mentioned the Goodman Pool, and the brothers' generous gift—eventually totaling $2.8 million—that made it possible.

"For six decades Madison debated a pool," Cieslewicz said, "but it took the Goodman brothers to make it happen. The Goodman Pool will live on as a testament to Irwin Goodman's community spirit and his understanding of the community he loved."

The story mentioned the Goodman Community Center, and the $2 million gift from the brothers that made its new location and greatly expanded programs possible. The Center's director, Becky Steinhoff, mentioned in an interview that Irwin once told her "the best exercise for the heart is bending down to lift a child."

Steve Morrison of the Madison Jewish Community Council was quoted: "Irwin Goodman has been truly a pillar of the Jewish community for close to eight decades. No one has had a greater impact."

Downtown Rotary executive director Pat Jenkins recalled how it was Irwin, along with Bob, who got the weekly luncheons to include a vegetarian dish of rice, beans and baked potato. The story mentioned Irwin's personal austerity, which was all the more striking in the context of their endless philanthropy. The reporters found an earlier quote from Irwin, talking about the 1950 Oldsmobile that he drove for more than 35 years (and eventually allowed to be auctioned for charity): "I had offers to sell it," Irwin said, "but, then, I'd just have to buy a new car for a lot more money and I doubt that it would take me across town any better than this one."

Irwin's death brought other tributes. Dave Zweifel, the quintessential Madison newspaperman, and a longtime friend, wrote about Irwin's philanthropy, but also mentioned the brothers' passion for sports, and not only, as some might have assumed, University of Wisconsin athletics.

"I remember visiting with them in their seats behind home plate at Warner Park in 1982, as the Oakland A's affiliate Madison Muskies made their season debut," Zweifel wrote. "They were among the first to buy season tickets to the Muskies and seldom missed a home game.

"They were also big fans of the Milwaukee Brewers," Zweifel continued. "Each year they invited me to join them at the Madison Dugout Club's annual baseball banquet, which they graciously supported. The banquet features appearances by many Brewer players. Irv's favorite back then was B. J. Surhoff, with whom the Goodmans became close friends. One summer I drove them to County Stadium to see a Brewers game and Surhoff's wife came over to chat before the game."

Two days later, Scott Milfred, editorial page editor of the *Wisconsin State Journal*, had a column about Irwin headlined: "Jeweler had heart of gold."

Milfred recalled how in 1998, as a young reporter, he had been assigned to interview the Goodmans and was astonished to find them living in a downtown apartment not much fancier than his own modest apartment across the street.

"Other than its spectacular view of Lake Monona," Milfred wrote in his tribute to Irwin, "their apartment was modest. And Irwin's sincerity, along with Bob's good humor, made it instantly clear during my first interview why they were so trusted and beloved.

"Their old-school business smarts, thrifty lifestyles and hearts of gold make it all possible.

"Try as I might," Milfred continued, "over weeks of reporting, I couldn't find anybody—not even other jewelers—who would say the slightest negative thing about them."

Irwin was buried at a private graveside service at Madison's Forest Hill Cemetery with perhaps 25 people in attendance. It was always going to be a small service, family and close friends. Irwin wanted it that way. He worked hard, too, in the months before his death, on the paid obituary that appeared in the *Wisconsin State Journal*

Bob (left) and Irwin, near their State Street store, on one of many days when they were honored in Madison.

ful as a hand reaching out to another in a gesture of support and human kindness. By this measure and many others, Irwin was a very successful man. Irwin lived his life according to his ideals of deep commitment to the people of this community. When asked about his extraordinary philanthropy, Irwin would always quickly mention his mother, Belle, explain that she was the inspiration of goodwill, and that she passed this on to him. Irwin found happiness in life through service to others, and his generosity will be remembered for generations to come."

The gravesite at Forest Hill Cemetery is in a clearing not far from the Glenway Golf Course, a green and peaceful open space amid a scattering of trees. Irwin's stone was placed adjacent to a larger "Goodman" stone. On the opposite side of the larger stone are the markers of his parents, Harry and Belle.

Rabbi Jonathan Biatch delivered a eulogy to the small group that gathered on Sept. 1, 2009. Near the end of his remarks, the rabbi said of Irwin:

"His personal lifestyle represented a modesty and humility that should be an example to us who live in the society of consumption that we have created. Living comfortably, and nowhere near their means, he and Bob showed us that one needs only to ensure one's health and comfort, and that the rest can return to do good work for others. . . .

May Irwin's life of service be an inspiration to those who come after him! May his modest style of life remind us and others to focus on appropriate lifetime priorities! And may his memory always be a blessing, for us and all future generations of the people of Madison!"

the morning of the service. The tone was modest but the accomplishments, read in total, were those of a giant. Unsurprisingly, Irwin had stressed his family's commitment to philanthropy, quoting Nelson Underwood: "The true meaning of life is to plant trees, under whose shade you do not expect to sit."

Later in the obituary, there was this:

"Success has many measures, but none so power-

Two weeks after Irwin's death, Tammy Baldwin stood up in the United States House of Representatives and gave a testimonial to Irwin in which she included Bob. Madison's congresswoman ended her remarks by saying, "Bob and Irwin Goodman shared far more than a bloodline. They shared an abiding commitment to each other and to their adopted hometown. I join the greater Madison community in honoring their life's work and loving spirit."

Certainly no one was more devastated by Irwin's death than Bob.

Their cousin Susan Hill attended Irwin's funeral and recalled how grief-stricken Bob appeared.

"Bob was just totally distraught," she said. "It was heart-wrenching to see. It was doubtful if Bob would be able to make it to the funeral, but he did."

Theirs had been a truly unique relationship, filled with love, respect, and, not insignificantly, all the attributes of a great friendship. They really did enjoy each other's company more than any other. Given the chance, Irwin would tout Bob's virtues, while Bob would tout Irwin's. Their friends might chuckle about it, but it was real.

For a time, those close to Bob resisted even mentioning Irwin's name, so overwhelming was the loss. Slowly, as weeks became months, that changed.

"Eventually Bob started talking about Irwin," Mary Rouse said. "He started telling jokes."

Still, no one close to Bob and Irwin, who had seen their interdependence, could have been shocked when, on April 1, 2010, a little more than eight months after Irwin's death, Bob Goodman died, at 90.

As was the case with Irwin's death the previous August, the passing of Bob Goodman was front page news in Madison.

George Hesselberg, a veteran and talented newspaper writer, began his *Wisconsin State Journal* piece on Bob with this: "Robert Goodman, 90, who with brother Irwin changed the face of Madison by bringing a smile to it, died Thursday."

Hesselberg continued: "Of the two, 'Bob' was the talkative, gregarious one, the one without the glasses. He told 'groaner' jokes, played softball, kept track on an index card of a customer's monthly payments for an engagement ring, and with his brother gave away money because it was the right thing to do."

The story mentioned the brothers' major philanthropic gifts, but also made a point of listing several smaller, lesser known gifts, which the Goodmans routinely made to little or no fanfare: $2,000 for the Capital City Band concerts; $1,000 for a golf outing for disabled students; $2,500 to the Combat Blindness Foundation; $2,000 to support students interested in technology; and $2,000 for a group of Edgewood College students to visit the National Holocaust Museum.

The Goodman Community Center's Becky Steinhoff said what most of the city was thinking: "They were incredibly humble, sweet and truly generous. They had truly made a decision to live modestly so they could make incredible gifts to the community. It was what made them happy."

Bob's paid obituary recalled his prowess as an athlete and noted that he would "be remembered for his kindness and generosity and for the care he demonstrated to our community." The balance of the obituary simply listed the Goodmans' philanthropic contributions, along with the individual awards Bob received over the years. Viewed together in print, the awards were breathtaking in their scope, the fruit of a life very well lived.

Bob Goodman was buried April 7, 2010, in a small private service in a grave next to Irwin's, near their parents, Harry and Belle, in Forest Hills cemetery. In his graveside eulogy Rabbi Jonathan Biatch said,

> "Bob was, similar to his brother Irwin, one of the most self-effacing people around. He shunned the spotlight, preferring to give credit for his accomplishments to others, and refusing many of the 'naming opportunities' that others offered him. He would only note that, with gratitude, he was able to help others, and that he was simply able to be the right place at the right time.
>
> He has been portrayed as someone who was vivacious and loquacious, the man who would greet you, the man who might be an extraordinary speaker, and someone who would extend his hand to you in greeting the first time he set eyes on you. And all of this persona—this Big Bob Goodman image that we carry with us—is true.
>
> Yet others would add that, in private, he was reserved and quiet, yet very involved in a direct way with the person to whom he was speaking. He appeared to be a bit circumspect, though when he was speaking with you his glance in your direction

Bob (left) and Irwin seated inside Monona Terrace, the Madison convention center not far from their downtown apartment.

always let you know he was thinking about you and nothing else. If you were there, you were the object of the moment, and no one else mattered."

In his *Wisconsin State Journal* news obituary of Bob, George Hesselberg wrote: "With Robert's death, the community loses an irreplaceable font of charm, but not necessarily money—thanks to the continuing Goodman Foundation."

The Goodman Foundation was established in December 1961, nearly a half century before the brothers' death, although, in their lifetime, it was not the major vehicle for their philanthropy.

With the deaths of Bob and Irwin, the bulk of their assets went to the foundation, which, as of 2013, was run by a board of four men with close professional and/or personal ties to the Goodmans: attorney Howard Sweet; certified public accountant E.G. Schramka; retired

UW–Madison business professor Robert Pricer; and the former executive director of the Jewish Federation of Madison, Steve Morrison.

After the brothers died, the board drafted a strategic plan for the foundation that included this mission statement:

"The Irwin A. and Robert D. Goodman Foundation is a charitable organization dedicated to preserving and enhancing the legacy of Irwin and Bob in Madison, Wisconsin by investing its resources in public recreation and fitness, the Jewish community, nutrition education and increased access to healthy foods, and organizations supported by Irwin and Bob in their lifetimes."

"They gave us some guidance," Howard Sweet said of

WISCONSIN STATE JOURNAL

TUESDAY, SEPTEMBER 1, 2009 • Madison's largest reporting team • Breaking news 24 hours a day at **www.madison.com**

OBITUARY | IRWIN GOODMAN, 94

Goodman's life of generosity, thrift

The United Way and the Jewish community were bolstered by jewelry store owner's charity.

By MATTHEW DeFOUR and WILLIAM R. WINEKE
Wisconsin State Journal

Irwin Goodman, a pillar of the Madison community who along with his brother, Robert, gave more than $10 million to philanthropic causes, died Sunday at his Madison home. He was 94.

Though he amassed his fortune selling jewelry, Goodman was able to give so much because of his frugal lifestyle, colleagues said.

"(Irwin) put most of his means toward the community, rather than his own life," United Way of Dane County President Leslie Howard said. "The community really was his child."

Goodman and his brother, Robert, oper-

ated Goodman's Jewelers at 220 State St., from 1937 until their retirement in 1998. Although each brother greeted customers warmly, Robert was pretty much the "outside" salesman and Irwin operated more behind the scenes, traveling the world to select diamonds and seeing to it the business

Please see **GOODWIN**, *Page A9*

Irwin Goodman's death in 2009 was front-page news in Madison.

Bob and Irwin. "They wanted us to support those organizations and areas that they had supported, and were important to them."

Sweet got to know the Goodmans when they called him with a piece of legal work. He was never exactly sure how they found him; it might have had something to do with Howard's dad having operated a grocery store on State Street not far from the jewelry store. But their relationship deepened and Sweet did the legal work of helping structure the large naming gifts late in the brothers' lives. His home was on a route Bob and Irwin often used for their daily walks. Sweet liked to play the piano and on summer days the brothers could hear the music through an open window.

"Irwin would wave," Sweet said. "Bob would stick his fingers in his ears."

The foundation has continued to make generous gifts throughout the Madison community, with an eye on their mission statement.

"Our goal," Sweet said, "is to try to enhance their legacy. Not only do what they would have done, but do it in a way that in the long run will enhance their memory."

In June, 2010, just two months after Bob's death in April, it was announced that the new South Madison Branch Library would be named for Bob and Irwin.

The Goodman Foundation made a gift of $250,000 to the capital campaign of the 12,000-foot library that opened that fall on South Park Street. The gift wouldn't have necessarily seemed to have fallen into the parameters mapped out by the foundation board in its mission statement, but it was clearly something of which Bob and Irwin would have approved.

Indeed, toward the end of their lives they had spoken about a gift to the library. The city was in serious negotiations to expand and enhance its downtown central branch. In the end, the timing wasn't quite right. But the foundation was pleased to provide a large gift to the south branch. Not only was it consistent with the Goodmans' desire late in their lives to help the library system, it also provided a major boost to the south Madison neighborhood, the neighborhood of the Goodman Pool, and helped to assure that the area would continue its positive growth. The Goodman library on South Park Street is a community center in its own right, filled with kids and parents, enjoying Bob's and Irwin's ongoing generosity.

On the east side, the Goodman Community Center has instituted an annual Goodman Days event to celebrate the center and remember the brothers who made it possible. The second celebration, in June 2011, drew more than 100 people, young and old, to the center. They

WISC... STATE JOURNAL

★★ SATURDAY, APRIL 3, 2010   •   Madison's largest reporting team   •   Breaking news 24 hours a day at www.madison.com

CHURCH SCANDAL

Priest likens criticism to anti-Semitism

By DANIEL J. WAKIN
and RACHEL DONADIO
The New York Times

ROME — A senior Vatican priest, speaking before Pope Benedict XVI at a Good Friday service, compared the world's outrage at sexual abuse scandals in the Catholic Church to the persecution of the Jews, prompting angry responses from victims' advocates and consternation from Jewish groups.

The Vatican spokesman quickly distanced the Vatican from the remarks, which came on the day Christians mark the Crucifixion. They underscored how much the Catholic Church has felt under...

In his front-page obituary of Bob Goodman in 2010, veteran newspaperman George Hesselberg wrote that Bob and Irwin "changed the face of Madison by bringing a smile to it."

ROBERT GOODMAN, 90

Generous, humble, caring

Businessman, benefactor praised

By GEORGE HESSELBERG
ghesselberg@madison.com
608-252-6140

Robert Goodman, 90, who with brother Irwin changed the face of Madison by bringing a smile to it, died Thursday.

Of the two, "Bob" was the talkative, gregarious one, the one without the glasses. He told "groaner" jokes, played softball, kept track on an index card of a customer's monthly payments for an engagement ring, and with his brother gave away money because it was the right thing to do.

The Goodmans lived frugally so they could give millions of dollars to charitable causes in Madison, where their generosity was both highly visible — a municipal swimming pool, a community center, a university softball field — and easily overlooked but highly valued: $20,000 for swimming lessons for the poor, $2,000 for the Capital City Band concerts, $1,000 for a golf outing for disabled students.

The Goodmans operated Goodman's Jewelers at 220 State St. from 1937 until their retirement in 1998. Robert was the talker, while Irwin operated more behind

Robert Goodman "was the extrovert."

the scenes. Privately, they lived together in an apartment on West Wilson Street, never married, and had no children. They were rarely seen apart, eating together, going to movies, watching their Mr. Bean tapes, choosing causes to support.

Irwin died last August at 94.

"Robert was the extrovert, Irwin was the introvert," said Becky Steinhoff, director of the Goodman Center, a bustling commu-

Please see **GOODMAN**, Page A6

---

ate ice cream, listened to music and heard a tribute to the two men who had done so much for the city of Madison.

One of the ice cream servers was Dewayne Powell, who had begun coming to the center in second grade and was by the summer of 2011, employed in its finance department. He also coached one of the center's youth basketball teams. He told the *State Journal* the hope was that reminding people of the Goodmans' philanthropic example would inspire those listening to also give back to the community, whether it be a financial contribution or volunteering their time.

In July, 2011, the month after the second Goodman Days celebration at the community center, the Goodman Pool on the other side of town for the first time entered a team in the All-City Swim Meet. The free swimming lessons provided by a gift from Bob and Irwin planted the seed, and continued support from the Goodman Foundation and other groups—most notably the Shelley Glover Sports Education Foundation—eventually made the swim team a reality. The Goodman Pool team consisted of 60

swimmers in 2011, half of them minorities.

In March 2012, the Beth Israel Center in Madison announced that the Goodman Foundation had pledged an initial gift of $1.5 million for the synagogue's proposed $5.5 million remodeling project. The foundation also pledged matching dollars up to an additional $500,000.

Other projects remain under consideration. The foundation has looked at trying to fund a tournament caliber softball complex, which was a dream of Bob Goodman's for Madison, but the right location and other details have not come together yet.

In October 2012, it was announced that the Goodman Foundation was donating more than $660,000 for synthetic turf at the showcase stadium in the Reddan Soccer Park in Verona. The Goodman Pitch, as the field is called, opened in 2013.

"That facility is well-organized and well-run," Goodman Foundation board member E.G. Schramka said. "There are large numbers of kids out there all the time."

The continued good work of the foundation and the

many successful buildings and other projects that bear the Goodman name should ensure that Bob and Irwin Goodman will be remembered in Madison, the city they came to in the 1930s and happily adopted as their own for more than 70 years.

Of course, Bob and Irwin are also remembered in the hearts and minds of those they touched personally. Some were close friends. Others may have had only the briefest of encounters—the purchase of a ring, or perhaps just a friendly wave on a daily walk—and yet continue to remember them fondly, moved by the natural good will that seemed to issue from Bob and Irwin like rays from the sun.

One of their oldest friends, Ghita Bessman, recalled going to visit them near the end, when they were ill and not getting out often from their Wilson Street apartment. Ghita had dropped off a package of some kind, and as she was leaving, she ran into a young woman who stepped out of a unit across the hall. Seeing Ghita knew the Goodmans, the young woman said how much it meant to her that whenever she encountered Bob and Irwin, they made a point of smiling and telling her how nice she looked.

"She said they made her feel beautiful," Ghita said.

Another good friend, Mary Rouse, found her own way to remember Bob and Irwin. Rouse had heard an elderly poet say on the radio that he was studying for a new vocation upon his death. He wanted to be a cloud.

In the piece on Bob and Irwin that Rouse did for the Jewish Social Services newsletter, she wrote, "I nominate the Goodman brothers to be beautiful clouds over Madison and Dane County, watching out for all of us."

Rouse sees them when she looks toward the sky on the kind of soft summer day when Madison is as beautiful as any place on Earth.

"Irwin is smiling," she wrote. "Bob is telling jokes."

ACKNOWLEDGMENTS

This book started several years ago with an invitation from Howard Sweet to share a cup of coffee.

Howard was, and is, on the board of the Goodman Foundation, which Bob and Irwin established in 1961. The board was interested in having a book written about Bob and Irwin.

That coffeehouse chat was the start of a long and largely enjoyable journey for me. I have never before researched a book, or even a long article, in which everyone approached agreed happily to be interviewed, and only had trouble finding enough good things to say about the subject at hand. I'm reminded of something Madison journalist and novelist Rob Zaleski told me during our interview. Zaleski wrote an excellent *Capital Times* profile of Bob and Irwin after being granted a rare in-depth interview with the brothers.

"Going into the interview, I was thinking that these guys couldn't possibly live up to their image," Rob said. "In fact, they exceeded it."

Thanks, then, to Howard Sweet and the other members of the foundation board—E.G. Schramka, Steve Morrison, and Bob Pricer—not only for the assignment, but for agreeing to be interviewed during my research. I should mention that Bob and Irwin's great friend, Mary Rouse, who I also interviewed for the book, recently joined the board.

Much of this book is based on original interviews, supplemented by archival newspaper and magazine articles. The individual stories are cited in the text, but I want to especially thank the *Wisconsin State Journal* and

The Capital Times and the journalists who reported on Bob and Irwin across their nearly 70 years in Madison. For the section on Irwin and Bob's extended family, I owe great thanks to Dee Grimsrud, a retired reference archivist at the Wisconsin Historical Society. Dee specializes in genealogy, and tracked down numerous documents—including the ship's log from when Bob's and Irwin's father first came to the United States—that assisted my research. The section would have been much less without her; any errors, of course, are my own.

For agreeing to be interviewed, along with those already mentioned, I thank the following people: Jack Stevenson, John Hayes, Susan Hill, Nino Amato, Dave Cieslewicz, Ghita Bessman, Joe Silverberg, Arlon Mason, Pat Richter, Paul Reilly, Barb Reilly, Dolores Tollefson, Tom Grannis, Gordon Derzon, Mark Huberman, Al Goldstein, Joel Minkoff, Joel Maturi, Leslie Ann Howard, Kathy Hubbard, Becky Steinhoff, Russ Hellickson, and Nancy Hellickson.

For help in the editing, design, and production process, I am grateful to Rosemary Zurlo-Cuva, Elisabeth Owens at UW–Madison Libraries' Parallel Press, and Earl Madden and Nancy Brower at University Marketing.

Finally, my wife, Jeanan Yasiri Moe, herself a former journalist, read the chapters in draft as they were written, made insightful comments, and didn't complain when her husband said he had to spend yet another weekend afternoon typing. My work on this book is dedicated to her.

INDEX